The best of poetry lond

The best of poetry london

Poetry and prose 1988–2013

Selected and edited by Tim Dooley and Martha Kapos

First published in Great Britain in 2014 by
Carcanet Press Limited
Alliance House
Cross Street
Manchester M2 7AQ

www.carcanet.co.uk

A CIP catalogue record for this book is available from
the British Library

ISBN 978 1 84777 249 7

The publisher acknowledges financial assistance from
Arts Council England

Typeset by XL Publishing Services, Exmouth

Printed and bound in England by SRP Ltd, Exeter

Contents

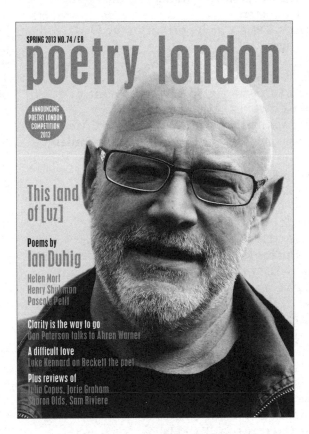

Acknowledgements

The editors and publisher gratefully acknowledge permission to reprint the following poems and articles in this book:

MONIZA ALVI: 'The Country at My Shoulder', 'A Bowl of Warm Air' from *Split World: Poems 1990–2005* (Bloodaxe, 2008); SIMON ARMITAGE: 'The Empire' (uncollected); MARIANNE BORUCH: ' It isn't that serious before dawn, trees' from *The Book of Hours*. Copyright © 2011 by Marianne Boruch. Reprinted with the permission of The Permissions Company, Inc. on behalf of Copper Canyon Press, www.coppercanyonpress.org; PAUL BATCHELOR: 'To a Halver' from *The Love Darg* (Clutag, 2014); EMILY BERRY: 'Zanzibar' from *Dear Boy* (Faber, 2013); LIZ BERRY: 'Bird' from her forthcoming collection (Chatto & Windus, 2014); CAROLINE BIRD: 'Wild Flowers' from *Watering Can* (Carcanet, 2009); CHARLES BOYLE, 'Writ in Water', part of 'The Office Suite' from *The Very Man* (Carcanet, 1993); ALISON BRACKENBURY: 'Calf Sound' from *Bricks and Ballads* (Carcanet, 2004) and 'Lapwings' from *Then* (Carcanet, 2013); COLETTE BRYCE: 'Self-Portrait in the Dark (with Cigarette)' from *Self-Portrait in the Dark* (Picador, 2008); CIARAN CARSON: 'The Redoubt' from *For All We Know* 2008 by kind permission of the author and The Gallery Press, Loughcrew, Oldcastle, County Meath, Ireland; US rights courtesy of Wake Forest University Press; JULIA COPUS: part of 'Ghost' from *The World's Two Smallest Humans* (Faber, 2012); FRED D'AGUIAR: 'S-Joe' from *Continental Shelf* (Carcanet, 2009); KWAME DAWES: 'Hawk' from *Midland*, 2001 by Kwame Dawes. Copyright © 2001 by Kwame Dawes. This material is used by permission of Ohio University Press, www.ohioswallow.com; NICHOLA DEANE: 'My Moriarty' from *My Moriarty* (Flarestack, 2012); GREG DELANTY: 'On Reading the Diaries of Christopher Columbus' (uncollected); MICHAEL DONAGHY: 'Defensible Positions' and 'May I Make A Suggestion?' from *The Shape of the Dance* (Picador, 2009); TIMOTHY DONNELLY: 'Apologies from the Ground Up' (uncollected); TIM DOOLEY: 'Working from Home' from *Imagined Rooms* (Salt, 2010); MARK DOTY: 'In their flight' from *School of the Arts* by Mark Doty (Cape, 2005). Copyright © 2005 by Mark Doty. Courtesy of Harper Collins Publishers. JANE DRAYCOTT: 'The Tor' from *The Night Tree* (Carcanet, 2004); CAROL ANN DUFFY: 'Scheherazade' from *The Bees* (Picador, 2012); IAN DUHIG: 'Blood' from *The Lammas Hireling* (Picador, 2003); HELEN DUNMORE: 'The Surgeon Husband' from *Bestiary* (Bloodaxe, 1977); ANGIE ESTES: 'Brief Encounter' and 'Shade' from *Enchantée* (Oberlin College Press, 2013); PAUL FARLEY: 'The Mobile Library's Last Stop' (uncollected) and 'Google Earth' from *The Dark Film* (Picador, 2012); ELAINE FEINSTEIN: 'A Visit' from *Talking to the Dead* (Carcanet, 2007); EAMON GRENNAN: 'Even under the rain…' from *The Quick of It* (2004) by kind permission of the author and The Gallery Press, Loughcrew, Oldcastle, County Meath, Ireland. Copyright © 2004 by Eamon Grennan. Reprinted with the permission of The Permissions Company, Inc., on behalf of Graywolf Press, Minneapolis, Minnesota, www.graywolfpress.org; PHILIP GROSS: 'Designs for a Water Garden' from *The Water Table* (Bloodaxe, 2009); MARILYN HACKER 'Glose: Willow' from *Names: Poems* by Marilyn Hacker. Copyright © by Marilyn Hacker. Used by permission of W.W. Norton & Co., Inc. *Essays on Departure* (Carcanet, 2006); DAVID HARSENT: 'Spatchcock' from *Night* (Faber, 2011); SEAMUS HEANEY: 'To Pablo Neruda in Tamlaghtduff' from *District and Circle* (Faber, 2006) by Seamus Heaney. Copyright © 2006 by Seamus Heaney. Reprinted by permission of Farrar, Straus and Giroux, LLC.; W.N. HERBERT: 'Mount Pelée' from *The Testament of the Reverend Thomas Dick* (Arc, 1994); SELIMA HILL: 'Sips' from *Trembling hearts in the bodies of dogs: New and Selected Poems* (Bloodaxe, 1994) and 'The Elephant Whose Sturgeon-Like Blood' from *The Best British Poetry* (Salt, 2012); MATTHEW HOLLIS: 'Isostacy' from *Groundwater* (Bloodaxe, 2004); KATHLEEN JAMIE: 'Hawk and Shadow' from *The Overhaul* (Picador, 2012); EMMA JONES: 'Pietà' from *The Striped World* (Faber, 2009); MARTHA KAPOS: 'The Wild Duck in the Attic' from *Supreme Being* (Enitharmon, 2008); BRIGIT PEGEEN KELLY: 'The Philosophers' (uncollected); MIMI KHALVATI: 'Carrying a Sheet of Glass' (uncollected); JOHN KINSELLA: 'Chainsaw' from *Peripheral Light: Selected and New Poems* by John Kinsella. Copyright © 2004 by John Kinsella. Used by permission of W.W. Norton & Company, Inc.; AUGUST KLEINZAHLER: 'The Tree' from *Live from the Hong Kong Nile Club* (Faber, 2000). Copyright © 2000 by August Kleinzahler. Reprinted by permission of Farrar, Straus and Giroux, LLC.; YUSEF KOMUNYAKAA: 'Astrea's Footnotes' from *Taboo: The Wishbone Trilogy, Part 1* (Farrar, Straus & Giroux, 2004). Copyright © 2004 by Yusef Komunyakaa. Reprinted by permission of Farrar, Straus and Giroux, LLC.; FRANCES LEVISTON: 'Sulis' from *Oxford Poets 2013* (Carcanet, 2013); JOHN McCULLOUGH: '!' (uncollected); MEDBH McGUCKIAN: 'The Meaning of Margaret's Hands' from *The High Caul Cap*, 2012 by kind permission of the author and The Gallery Press, Loughcrew, Oldcastle, County Meath, Ireland; US rights courtesy of Wake Forest University Press; JAMIE McKENDRICK: 'King Billy's Nemesis' from *Out There* (Faber, 2012); DORA MALECH, 'Fair Play' from *Shore Ordered Ocean* (Waywiser, 2009); BILL MANHIRE: 'Velvet' from *Selected Poems* (Carcanet, 2014); E.A. MARKHAM: 'Taxis' from *Looking Out, Looking In* (Anvil, 2007); KATHRYN MARIS: 'Street Sweeper' from *God*

Loves You (Seren, 2013); TOBY MARTINEZ DE LAS RIVAS: 'Covenant' (uncollected); STANLEY MOSS: 'Babies' from *Songs of Imperfection* (Anvil, 2004) and from *God Breaketh Not All Men's Hearts Alike: New and Later Collected Poems.* Copyright © 2011 by Stanley Moss. Reprinted with the permission of The Permissions Company, Inc., on behalf of Seven Stories Press, www.sevenstories.com; SINÉAD MORRISSEY: 'The Second Lesson of the Anatomists' from *The State of the Prisons* (Carcanet, 2005); HELEN MORT: 'Rope' (uncollected); PAUL MULDOON: 'Old Country V' from *Horse Latitudes* (Faber, 2006) by Paul Muldoon. Copyright © 2006 by Paul Muldoon. Reprinted by permission of Farrar, Straus and Giroux, LLC.; LES MURRAY: 'The Ice Indigene' from *Conscious and Verbal* (Carcanet, 1999) (Snellgrove & Duffy, 2000); DALJIT NAGRA: 'Darling and Me' from *Look, We Have Coming To Dover!* (Faber, 2007); CRISTINA NEWTON: 'Edison Peña Runs the Six Miles' from *Cry Wolf* (Templar Poetry, 2012); EILÉAN NÍ CHUIL-LÉANAIN: 'Dream Shine' (uncollected); D. NURKSE: 'The Evacuation Corridor' from *Burnt Island* by D. Nurkse. Used by permission of Alfred A. Knopf, an imprint of Knopf Doubleday Publishing Group, a division of Random House LLC. All rights reserved. And 'Attrition' (uncollected); SEAN O'BRIEN: 'The Lost Book' from *November* (Picador, 2011); SHARON OLDS: 'Satin Maroon' from *One Secret Thing* by Sharon Olds (Cape, 2009). Copyright © 2008 by Sharon Olds. 'Sleekit Cowrin' from *Stag's Leap* by Sharon Olds (Cape, 2012). Copyright © 2012 by Sharon Olds. Used by permission of Alfred A. Knopf, an imprint of Knopf Doubleday Publishing Group, a division of Random House LLC. All rights reserved. ALICE OSWALD: 'Dunt' from *Spacecraft Voyager 1: New and Selected Poems.* Copyright © 2007 by Alice Oswald. Reprinted with the permission of The Permissions Company, Inc., on behalf of Graywolf Press, Minneapolis, Minnesota, www.graywolfpress.org; PASCALE PETIT: 'Mirador' from *Heart of a Deer* (Enitharmon, 1998) and 'What the Water Gave Me VI' from *What the Water Gave Me: Poems after Frida Kahlo* (Seren, 2010); HEATHER PHILLIPSON: 'Oh. Is he dead?' from *Instant-flex 718* (Bloodaxe, 2013); KATHERINE PIER-POINT: 'Buffalo Calf' (uncollected); JACOB POLLEY: 'The Cheapjack' from *Little Gods* (Picador, 2006); PETER REDGROVE: 'Who is the higher penis here?' from *A Speaker for the Silver Goddess* (Stride, 2003); MAURICE RIORDAN: 'A Word from the Loki' from *A Word from the Loki* (Faber, 1995) and 'Faun Whistling to a Blackbird' from *The Water Stealer* (Faber, 2013); SAM RIVIERE: part of '81 Austerities' from *81 Austerities* (Faber, 2012); ROBIN ROBERTSON: 'The Plague Year' from *The Wrecking Light* (Picador, 2010); NEIL ROLLINSON: 'The Ecstasy of St Saviours Avenue' from *A Spillage of Mercury* (Cape, 1996); VALÉRIE ROUZEAU: 'Vain Poem' from *Talking Vrouz* (Arc, 2013); CAROL RUMENS: 'Little Epic' from *Blind Spots* (Seren, 2008); TOMAŽ ŠALAMUN: 'Nations' and 'Grandfather' (uncollected); JO SHAPCOTT: 'I am Contemplated by a Portrait of the Divine' from *Her Book* (Faber, 2000) and 'Somewhat Unravelled' from *Of Mutability* (Faber, 2010); KATHRYN SIMMONDS: 'Sunday at the Skin Launderette' from *Sunday at the Skin Launderette* (Seren, 2008); KEN SMITH: 'Narrow Road Deep North' from *Shed* (Bloodaxe, 2002); KAREN SOLIE: 'Spiral' from *The Living Option* (Bloodaxe, 2013); JEAN SPRACK-LAND: 'The Light Collector' from *Hard Water* (Cape, 2003); SAVIANA STANESCU: 'The Infanta Isabella' (uncollected); MARIA STEPANOVA: '(as they must)' (uncollected); JULIAN STANNARD: 'Don't Die' from *The Parrots of Villa Gruber Discover Lapis Lazuli* (Salmon, 2011); MICHAEL SYMMONS ROBERTS: 'Man in Fox Suit' / 'Fox in Man Suit' from *The Half-Healed* (Cape, 2008), US, Canada, Philippines rights granted by United Agents, www.unitedagents.co.uk; TOON TELLEGEN: 'A Man and an Angel' from *A Man and an Angel* (Shoestring, 2013); CHASE TWICHELL: 'Savin Rock' from *Horses Where the Answers Should Have Been: New and Selected Poems* (Bloodaxe, 2010). Copyright © 2010 by Chase Twichell. Reprinted with the permission of The Permissions Company, Inc., on behalf of Copper Canyon Press, www.coppercanyonpress.org; JACK UNDERWOOD: 'Wilderbeast' (uncollected); SCOTT VERNER: 'To Listen, Barefoot' (uncollected); JAN WAGNER: 'from 18 Pies' from *Achtzehn Pasteten* (Berlin Verlag, 2007); AHREN WARNER: part of 'Metousiosis' from *Pretty* (Bloodaxe, 2013); SUSAN WICKS: 'Lebküchen Haus' (uncollected); C.K. WILLIAMS: 'Jew on Bridge' from *Wait* (Bloodaxe, 2010 and Farrar, Straus and Giroux, 2010). Copyright © 2010 by C.K. Williams. Reprinted by permission of Farrar, Straus and Giroux, LLC.; SAMANTHA WYNNE-RHYDDERCH: 'Vive la Résistance!' from *Banjo* (Picador, 2012); YANG LIAN: 'Concentric Circles' from *Concentric Circles* (Bloodaxe, 2005); TAMAR YOSELOFF: 'Biology' from *Sweetheart* (Slow Dancer, 1998); MATTHEW ZAPRUDER: 'To Sergio Franchi' from *Sun Bear.* Copyright © 2014 by Matthew Zapruder. Reprinted with the permission of The Permissions Company, Inc., on behalf of Copper Canyon Press, www.coppercanyonpress.org.; RAÚL ZURITA: 'from INRI: The Sea' from *Inri*, translated by William Rowe. Copyright © 2009 by Raúl Zurita. Translation copyright © by William Rowe. Reprinted with the permission of The Permssions Company, Inc., on behalf of Marick Press, www.marickpress.com.

Every effort has been made to trace the copyright holders of the poems published in this book. The editors and publishers apologise if any material has been included without the appropriate acknowledgement, and will be glad to correct any oversights in future editions.

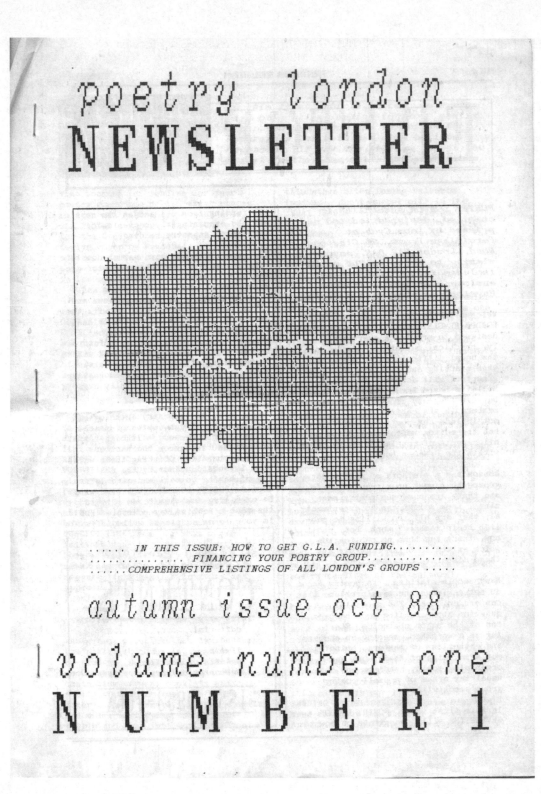

poetry london
NEWSLETTER

...... IN THIS ISSUE: HOW TO GET G.L.A. FUNDING..........
.... FINANCING YOUR POETRY GROUP..............
......COMPREHENSIVE LISTINGS OF ALL LONDON'S GROUPS .....

autumn issue oct 88

volume number one
NUMBER 1

At the Heart of Things:
Twenty-five Years of *Poetry London*

'The great turn-of-the-century poems are there to be written', wrote Maurice Riordan in an article for *Poetry London* in 1994. Such optimism about the potential of the new may be a necessary characteristic for those of us who find ourselves at one time or another involved in the production of poetry magazines. An early editor of *Poetry* magazine had as her motto, 'Yesterday's poet, whom we love, is not the one we are looking for'. Such a view doesn't necessarily imply a naïve belief in progress or a disregard for the past; it can also invoke a wary watchfulness for what in the fast-moving current of the present is worth salvaging or giving space to. To maintain an audience, a magazine needs to keep convincing its readers that it has a sense of what is important and alive – to quote Riordan's article again, 'Risk, speculative energy, a sense of adventure – these are what it's going to be about'.

Poetry London celebrated its twenty-fifth birthday in October 2013, straddling the turn of the century and attaining a milestone not many independent poetry magazines expect to reach. Its origins were comparatively modest. *Poetry London Newsletter* was founded by Leon Cych in 1988 as a 'forum and bulletin board' for those involved in running poetry events (readings, workshops, creative writing classes) across the capital's boroughs. It both signalled and responded to the growth of grassroots poetic activity among a generation of writers keen to learn from each other and become their own experts. Leon Cych was one of a group of poets who met in the Notting Hill flat of the Irish poet Robert Greacen and later at the Lamb in Bloomsbury. This group led by Matthew Sweeney included, along with several other poets who would make an impact in the years to come, Michael Donaghy, Jo Shapcott, Maurice Riordan, Charles Boyle and myself – each of whom would contribute poems or reviews to the magazine in its early years.

Pascale Petit was at the heart of another network of poets in the east of London. Within a year she and Moniza Alvi had joined Leon Cych as co-editors, and *Poetry London Newsletter* had expanded to include poems and book reviews as well as features, among them an occasional gossip column, 'Blather', providing *Private Eye*-style 'revelations' about institutions such as the Poetry Society or the London Arts Board. From the start the magazine mixed serious, informed writing with the quirky and unconventional. The September 1989 issue (the first to go beyond its listings mandate) included an essay on Mandelstam, a review by Lawrence Norfolk, and an account by Matthew Sweeney of a writing workshop in Highgate Cemetery.

The poems carried in early issues of the magazine reflected the multiculturalism of the capital and the growing significance of women's writing. An editorial from May 1991 made a conscious link between these areas. Regretting the restrictions women were still finding in reaching an audience unless their writing conformed to models prescribed by 'male editors', it argued that 'women have new areas to map' and 'are looking elsewhere for role models... to poetry from abroad, or to English poetry with roots in other cultures'. That desire to 'look elsewhere' was soon evident in the content of the magazine as it looked outside the capital for poems from emerging independent talents such as Selima Hill and W.N. Herbert and outside the UK in its reviews and features (the January 1992 issue, for example, included a report on the Harbourfront reading series in Toronto from the Nigerian poet Niyi Osundare). Reflecting on the early days of the magazine, Pascale Petit comments that her main aim was

> to publish the best poems I could find or that I was sent, and also to present a spectrum of poetry from poets in other cultures, some of it in translation. I don't think there was so much poetry in translation available then, and like Ted Hughes I felt it was essential to have access to it.

The production process of *Poetry London Newsletter* had the hand-to-mouth, samizdat enthusiasm typical of the 'little magazine' of its era. Early issues were typeset on Amstrad and Gateway 2000 word-processors, then duplicated using a photocopier and stapled by hand. Moniza Alvi recalls this period well:

I remember the three of us duplicating, collating and stapling, walking round and round a set of tables in a primary school hall, the separate pages of the *Newsletter* piled dauntingly high. There was at least one crisis on the production side and final copies could be less than perfect, but we were always immensely proud of the magazine and felt that the publication was respected and had a unique identity.

She also recalls the sense of achievement as the magazine grew, making such laborious tasks seem worthwhile:

When Pascale and I joined Leon, we hoped to give more prominence to the poetry section. At first we didn't have today's quantity of poetry submissions (we sat down together and read them in a day or so), but the publication was well reputed and we always found sufficient fine poems to make a strong issue. We showcased the poems by giving them plenty of space and a bold presentation, aiming for quality rather than quantity. The poetry section soon grew and the magazine became ever more clearly the forerunner of the one we have now. We were excited to be 'at the heart of things', to play a part in the fast-growing poetry scene in London and nationwide, the beginnings of a kind of poetry explosion. It's been marvellous to witness the way the magazine has gone from strength to strength, fulfilling so richly, more than fulfilling, the vision of those early years.

By 1996 Moniza Alvi and Leon Cych had left the magazine to concentrate on other projects and the editorial team had been enhanced by the arrival of Katherine Gallagher, Peter Daniels and Tamar Yoseloff. The magazine was relaunched that summer, professionally printed, with a commissioned design from Vici MacDonald and distribution by Central Books. The masthead title was now *Poetry London*, with *Newsletter* reduced to a strapline before disappearing entirely in 1999, at which point the magazine also began a tradition of using a monochrome photograph of a featured poet on its cover. Issues henceforth came regularly three times a year and were numbered consecutively rather than by notional volume. Editorial roles became more precise, with Pascale Petit leading as Poetry Editor, Tamar Yoseloff (and later Greta Stoddart) in charge of features and reviews, Peter Daniels managing listings and production and Katherine Gallagher promotions. Tamar Yoseloff has said that this greater professionalism 'shifted us from being a grassroots project to becoming a proper magazine and meant that readers could finally purchase the magazine through shops... Of course we never could have imagined the magazine would still be going now, but perhaps those significant steps ensured its future growth'.

Under these editors, the magazine (while retaining a distinctive vanguard feel) began to be less the voice of a particular generation of poets and more representative of the poetry world as a whole. Younger poets such as Paul Farley, John Kinsella and Jane Duran had early work published in the magazine and there were reviews by the then little-known Toby Litt. At the same time, more established writers such as Ruth Padel, Alison Brackenbury and Dennis O'Driscoll were featured, followed by major figures on the international stage such as Les Murray, August Kleinzahler and Kwame Dawes. Live events, which had accompanied launches of the magazine intermittently since National Poetry Day 1994, became regular features at a range of venues in London. I remember being asked by *Poetry London* to read with, among others, Khan Singh Kumar (a young poet from a South Asian background now better known as Daljit Nagra) in the rediscovered Old Operating Theatre above a church near St Thomas's Hospital, where we were assured the young Keats would have trained as a surgeon. Launch readings at Foyles Bookshop and more recently at the South Bank Centre have continued to be a key element in the magazine's range of activities.

Scott Verner became Reviews and Features Editor of *Poetry London* in 1999 after a career in advertising and public relations in Philadelphia and London. He remained in that role until I took over from him in 2008 and had a considerable influence on the magazine's shape and its fortunes. He was a formidable figure whose passion and determination were seen in tireless pursuit of funding applications and scrupulous concern for detail. He shared Pascale Petit's internationalist vision and this was reflected in a special feature by Stephen Watts spread over two issues, surveying poets living in London writing in languages other than English, as well as essay-length articles on Neruda, Vallejo and translation from the Chinese. From his editorship onwards, each issue would contain reviews of first collections and of poetry in translation and there would be regular features on poetry chapbooks and major figures from earlier in the modern period. The magazine also started to feature interviews with leading poets, initially conducted by John Stammers and Kathryn Maris, a practice that has become a regular feature in recent issues.

Pascale Petit remained as Poetry Editor until Spring 2005. In many ways her sixteen-year editorship defined the feeling of the magazine. *Poetry London* seemed to attract writing of a particularly vivid and imaginatively varied kind: poems with a strong sense of the body or of place but with an unfamiliar consciousness or sensitivity, oddly populated poems that, in her words, 'create (their) own world'. Martha Kapos commented on this phenomenon in the editorial to Pascale's final issue:

> The poems that have found their way into *Poetry London* may often bring with them an accompanying mixture of contradictory states of mind – a sense of rightness, but also a sense of shock, a sense of newness, but also of recognition, of something never seen or known before. So the poem is experienced as an invention, but paradoxically also as a discovery.

Martha Kapos had joined the magazine in 2001 as Assistant Poetry Editor, selecting the poems for one issue a year. Her issues brought many more US poets into the magazine and have helped make *Poetry London* one of the few magazines on either side of the Atlantic committed to bridging the gap between those divided by a common language. Her long-term commitment to the magazine has been an essential element in the continuity of its independent vision.

As Poetry Editor from 2005 to 2009, Maurice Riordan put a great deal of energy into securing the magazine's future, helping it gain regular funding status from the Arts Council and establishing the magazine as a charity with a board of trustees. His status as a poet attracted major figures such as Seamus Heaney to the magazine, while his nose for new talent introduced younger writers such as Jack Underwood, Frances Leviston and Paul Batchelor; under his editorship up to a third of the poems published in *Poetry London* came from writers yet to publish a first collection.

Following Maurice, Colette Bryce did just as much to enhance the magazine's prestige. When Roddy Lumsden commented in *The Best British Poetry 2011* that under her editorship '*Poetry London* has flourished with a variety and quality unmatched by any other publication', he was confirming that the magazine had become recognised as an authority on contemporary poetry while retaining its element of vitality and surprise. Its reputation is now secure as one of the more respected poetry magazines in the English-speaking world. Sean O'Brien has described it as 'essential reading', finding its treatment of contemporary poetry 'urgent and coherent', while Carol Ann Duffy calls *Poetry London* 'the poetry magazine I most want to read'.

Poetry London enters its second quarter-century as it entered its first, at a time when there is a vibrant new generation of poets trying to redefine their relationship with their art. The magazine has been privileged to publish early and important poems by Sam Riviere, Emily Berry, Liz Berry and John McCullough in its pages, as well as review articles by Luke Kennard, Helen Mort, Tom Chivers and others. Its new Poetry Editor, Ahren Warner, is a key member of that generation of poets and is already known to *Poetry London* readers as a reviewer, poet and interviewer. With him as a welcome part of our team, the magazine looks confidently ahead, knowing that the great poems of the mid-century may be out there waiting for us.

Tim Dooley, Reviews Editor
October 2013

MONIZA ALVI

The Country at My Shoulder

There's a country at my shoulder,
growing larger – soon it will burst,
rivers will spill out, run down my chest.

My cousin Azam wants visitors to play
ludo with him all the time.
He learns English in a class of seventy.

And I must stand to attention
with the country at my shoulder.
There's an execution in the square –

The women's dupattas are wet with tears.
The offices have closed
for the white-hot afternoon.

But the women stone-breakers chip away
at boulders, dirt on their bright hems.
They await the men and the trucks.

I try to shake the dust from the country,
smooth it with my hands.
I watch Indian films –

Everyone is very unhappy,
or very happy,
dancing garlanded through parks.

I hear of bribery, family quarrels,
travellers' tales – the stars
are so low you think you can touch them.

Uncle Aqbar drives down the mountain
to arrange his daughter's marriage.
She's studying Christina Rossetti.

When the country bursts, we'll meet.
Uncle Kamil shot a tiger,
it hung over the wardrobe, its jaws

fixed in a roar – I wanted to hide
its head in a towel.
The country has become my body –

I can't break bits off.
The men go home in loose cotton clothes.
In the square there are those who beg –

And those who beg for mercy.
Azam passes the sweetshop,
names the sugar monuments Taj Mahal.

I water the country with English rain,
cover it with English words.
Soon it will burst, or fall like a meteor.

III ii (June 1992)

JO SHAPCOTT

I'm Contemplated by a Portrait
of a Divine

I cannot speak to you. My lips are fused
where an archangel kissed them. I have never
made much of myself although I know,
sometimes, that space is touching me
because I have seen the crack in the universe
through which the galaxies stream. O God,
I will always know how to walk, no rest, until
it just ends in blackness when I fall down flat.
I have one arching eyebrow: my whole life
is in that eyebrow where an angel nestles
at the root of every hair, raising it up.
Dear Christ, I can hear vice rushing through
the grass. There is someone here.
If I could lick the glass
clean from this side, I might see her, though
I already know she would look the way
I want my soul to look. This pose
which I strain to keep, in which I lean
on the desk for dear life, is not a pose.
It's so important for keeping the drawer shut
in case my heart should slip out, fly up.

III iii (November 1992)

CHARLES BOYLE

Writ in Water

Across from our office was another
like ours, but whose whole façade
was made of glass. No pane was
exactly true, and on clear mornings our late
arrivals, hangovers, feet
on desks and industrious moments
were reflected there as if in water.

Later, when they switched on their lights,
the glass gave way
like the front of an old dolls' house.
There were the serious men in suits
and the secretaries at their keyboards,
and the man who clears memos from out-trays
to distribute to in-trays.

A vent at the top uttered steam and,
one day in early spring, a brimming froth of suds
which the lightest breeze creamed off.

I iv (September 1989)

W.N. HERBERT

Mont Pelée

*Blok and Bely, and others like them, believed that the
turn of the century coincided with the beginning of a
new era, marked by several signs, not least of which was
the passing of Solovyov.*
    Peter McCarty, *Hugh MacDiarmid and the Russians*

A glass of tea is shattering like consonants
under the weight of impassioned utterance.
The poets were just beginning to sober up, after
the afternoon's vodka and *sobornost*,
moving about under the hulk of Solovyov's thought
as momentarily bright
as fish through sliced light.
Now Mont Pelée has, swifter than the news
of its eruption, touched their evening's sky
with its bloody fingerprint.
Now they are staring through one eye;
the sunset's unfamiliar leap has reconciled
all their neat oppositions.
The glow is more than red from beyond
the world's bend, those familiar forges tucked there
gradually becoming bear, fire-claw. This
opacity is streaked and somehow lurid, like
a brilliant hare's fur glaze.

This expands their thought's type, prints
the horizon: their philosophy forms
a brightness there, dwelling
within the brightness. The broken glass is still
descending, irises have started to splay
from a vase knocked by
Blok's hand, as though he flung them from
his fingertips: all this simulates this inside-
outing of their brains.
They are rising spontaneously, as
you greet an unknown woman at a reception, as
a man does, shot in the nape, the guts
of thought dispersed upon this sky.
They are reading Solovyov's one name
for knowledge: *Sofia*. They are reading her
divine hips, her understanding thighs;

one breast is nippled harshly with the sun
as God's awareness must be, thrust into
this scoriating realm.
What they now see is dust, no more, aspersed
by a volcano. The mistake is as familiar as
a misheard name. What they will now write
comes from these orange billowings, earth's
scattering its blood and bowels.

                    III iv (May 1993)

SELIMA HILL

Sips

They come from certain over-heated quarries
that operate illicitly, in relays,
for those who are attracted to the flowers
that grow gigantic in the noonday sun.

And then they come on here and pester me –
sort of pester, sort of guide my lips
until, like them, I learn to sip the flowers
that grow so big they block the daylight out,

and people are condemned to live in darkness;
and, such is their confusion, every day
men with yellow dogs patrol the rocks
and kill and quarter anything that moves.

                    IV ii (May 1994)

MAURICE RIORDAN

A Word from the Loki

The Loki tongue does not lend itself
to description along classical lines.
Consider the vowels: there are just four,
including one produced by inspiration
(i.e. indrawn breath), which then requires
an acrobatic feat of projection
to engage with its troupe of consonants.
The skilled linguist can manage, at best,
a sort of tattoo; whereas the Loki
form sounds of balletic exactness.
Consider further: that the tribe has evolved
this strenuous means of articulation
for one word, a defective verb
used in one mood only, the optative.

No semantic equivalent can be found
in English, nor within Indo-European.
Loosely, the word might be glossed as *to joke*
provided we cite several other usages,
such as *to recover from snakebite;*
to eat fish with the ancestors;
to die at home in the village, survived
by all of one's sons and grandsons.
It is prohibited in daily speech,
and the Loki, a moderate people
who abjure physical punishments,
are severe in enforcing this taboo,
since all offenders, of whatever age
or status, are handed over to *mouri*

– sent, in effect, to a gruesome death:
for the victim is put on board a raft,
given a gourd of drinking water, a knife
and one of those raucous owl-faced
monkeys as companion, then towed
to midstream and set loose on the current.
Yet the taboo is relaxed at so-called

'joke parties': impromptu celebrations
that can be provoked by multiple births
or by an out-of-season catch of bluefish.
They are occasions for story-telling
and poetry, and serve a useful end
in allowing the young to learn this verb
and to perfect its exact delivery.

For the word is held to have come down
from the ancestral gods, to be their one gift.
And its occult use is specific: to ward off
the Loordhu, a cannibalistic horde,
believed to roam the interior forest,
who are reputed to like their meat
fresh and raw, to keep children *in lieu* of pigs,
and to treat eye and tongue as delicacies.
The proximity of danger is heralded
by a despondency that seems to strike
without visible cause but which effects
a swift change among a people by nature
brave and practical, bringing to a stop
in a matter of hours all work, play, and talk.

At such crises, the villagers advance
to the riverbank and, as night falls,
they climb into the trees, there to recite
this verb throughout the hours of darkness.
But since, in the memory of the village,
the Loordhu have never yet attacked,
one has reason to doubt the existence
of an imminent threat to the Loki –
who nevertheless continue, in suspense, their chant.
At once wistful and eerie, it produces
this observable result: that it quells
the commotion of the guenon monkeys
and lulls, within its range, the great forest.

III iii (November 1992)

MIMI KHALVATI

Carrying a sheet of glass in high wind

If only I could have
   flown with it as it bore
me up, ballast to my wing

of glass, insistence poised
   on the diving-board, my own voice
groaning yes – yes –

yes – on the door-plane, wheel-
   plane on the table-plane
swirled to become

a gyre of light
   in the flats and vortices
of space

but floored in a maze of
   routes and gifts and listed
tasks we only half-swirled

on each upward gust
   faced four winds at
crossroads and hugged low walls

as an east
   wind came, crossed to scupper
a west.   One hand free

one twice removed
   from the cutting-edge in
newspaper and glove

we homed my wing and I
   and half-way home my right
took charge

of a transparency I would hold
   head-high through which
we climbed the stairs.

(Oh we knew what flying
   felt like, how grave
its force, wild its bent

through street-grids, dance-steps
   on the cusp
of feather-fragments

between the fixity of will
   and wilfulness of wind we knew
as fear became elation

how the groundswell
   at our elbow, if yielded
to, ascends.)

V i (Summer 1995)

TIM DOOLEY

Working from Home

Watching through the open
French doors and conservatory glass, these birds queuing
at the feeder, pecking
and spitting out nuts and seeds, submissively anointing
their forefeathers
in the drinking bowl, I tidy a table, content with
what's brought us here:
times of waiting or worry, or losing our patience,
and days like these
when someone takes the children out and someone stays
with papers to read.
One day you're at the wave-pool. Spread out on the floor
are coursework folders:
teenage fiction, research on street-gangs, someone's response
to Wesker's *Roots*
and Hamid's painful, broken story of escaping from Tehran.
Shootings, disappearances,
a Pepsi Cola lorry overturned, unclean, its sticky bubbly fluid
running in the streets.
Another day you're working. In the Science Museum
Sam, Benedict and I
start the combine harvester, make counterweights for bridges
or launch a rocket.
Inside one case an Edsel; further on the crooked foot-digger
Hebridean crofters
called a caschcrom. By raising or lowering a handle,
those too poor to plough
determined the depth of the groove they needed to cut
in the sparse soil,
then gripped the wooden shaft and kick-started the share.

I was writing some review
that Saturday you and the children went to London Zoo.
Waiting in line
for llama rides, you thought you recognised the smiling, neat
and prematurely balding man
holding his son's hand just ahead, steadying him in the cart.
It turned out not to be,
you realised on the train coming home, another parent
from the local school,
but the man who'd won the Booker Prize for *Midnight's Children*.

That was years ago, of course,
and now you're upstairs writing a reference for a nurse
in your Literature class,
while I chop onions and listen for our not quite warring sons.

Though the author of *Shame*
might fear to be seen with a child in public now, though the enclosing,
impoverishing mind
shouts 'Kill the Ba'hais' or plans forced migrations, at evening
perennial birdsong
brightens our garden. It doesn't make everything right, but
makes it easier,
the children bathed and read to, easier to touch another's hand,
or speak quietly,
so when night does come what we notice is an arc of moonlight
curved by the ribbed
plastic roof above us – no rainbow or triumphal arch, but
what work tends toward –
efforts of love: attention, desire, holding darkness at bay.

III iii (November 1992)

MONIZA ALVI

A Bowl of Warm Air

Someone is falling towards you
as an apple falls from a branch,
moving slowly, imperceptibly as if
into a new political epoch,
or excitedly like a dog towards a bone.
He is holding in both hands
everything he knows he has –
a bowl of warm air.

He has sighted you from afar
as if you were a dramatic crooked tree
on the horizon and he has seen you close up
like the underside of a mushroom.
But he cannot open you like a newspaper
or put you down like a newspaper.

And you are satisfied that he is veering towards you
and that he is adjusting his speed
and that the sun and the wind and rain are in front of him
and the sun and the wind and rain are behind him.

V i (Summer 1995)

E.A. MARKHAM

Taxis

And you know some things seem to be passed down
through the family, like being in the army
or claiming a favourite grandmother's illness:
they say, once, the ruler of a country instead of killing
people, like his father, made an enemy of the flowers;
the smell upset him. When the country was rid of blooms
he discovered what made him nauseous was new paint
applied whenever he visited a school or factory.

But taxis were the things to bring tears
to our eyes. When her first driver smiled
and he had bad teeth, she felt cheated,
like flying to America in a second class train
with waitress service. The last time she cried in a taxi
was the night a man wanted to share, and she said no.

V ii (Autumn 1995)

PAUL FARLEY

The Mobile Library's Last Stop

Don't park it outside the World's End Estate –
instead, take it down to the Embankment,
idle in neutral like a suicide then roll
over the edge, the books sliding down shelves,
to hang weightless at the moment you tip,
in silhouette a Brandt nocturne of a bus
beginning its crawl over Battersea Bridge.

Watch the river fill the windscreen,
the cockpit dissolve in a fountain of glass
on impact – survive this to tread effluvia
as it fills, sharing a dwindling pocket
of air with the books, whose pages fold
and flap and glow, their ink as bold
as the day they rolled into this world.

24 (Summer 1996)

HELEN DUNMORE

The Surgeon Husband

Here at my worktop, foil-wrapping a silver salmon
– yes, a whole salmon – I am thinking
of the many bodies of women
that my husband daily opens.

Here he lunges at me in Wellingtons.
He is up to his armpits, a fisherman
tugging against the strength of the current.

I imagine the light for him, clean,
and a green robing of willow
and the fish hammering upstream.

I too tug at the flaps of the salmon
where its belly was, trying to straighten
the silver seams before they are sewn.
We are one in our dreams.

The epidural is patchy, his assistant's
handwriting is slipping. At eleven fifteen
they barb their patient to sleep, jot 'Knife to skin',
and the nurse smiles over her mask at the surgeon.

But I am quietly dusting out the fish-kettle,
and I have the salmon clean as a baby
grinning at me from the table.

IV iii (October 1994)

NEIL ROLLINSON

The Ecstasy of St Saviours Avenue (Valentine's Night)

Tonight the tenement smells of oysters
and semen, chocolate and rose petals.
The windows of every flat are open
to cool us, the noise of our limberings
issues from every sash as if the building
was hyperventilating in the cold
February air. We can hear the moans
of the Rossiters, the Hendersons,
the babysitters in number 3; a gentle
pornography rousing us like an aphrodisiac.
For once the house is harmonious, we rock
in our beds; our rhythms hum
in the stone foundations.
                    We shall have to be careful;
like soldiers who must break step on a bridge.
We stagger our climaxes one by one,
from the basement flat to the attic room,
a pounding of mattresses moves through the house
in a long, multiple, communal orgasm.
The building sighs like a whorehouse.
We lie in our sheets watching the glow
of street lights colour the sky; the chimneys
blow their smoke like the mellow exhalations
of post-coital cigarettes.

V iii (Spring 1996)

SCOTT VERNER

To Listen, Barefoot

Crushed oyster shells are what her voice reminds me of.
I don't mean rough, but that surprising density
of something layered, both soft and sharp at once
studded dark with iridescence
the spray of an ocean wave caught and made solid.

We lay down oyster shells on boondock dirt tracks
that hit out through sawgrass and palmetto scrub
past cottonmouths and golden slipper egrets
from wayback hummocks and cypress swamps
to stop the ruts and backbone-busting corrugations
a sandy road is liable to take on in time.
And they're cool to walk on in the heat of the day
giving it right back where it comes from.
Such a path can lead me anywhere.

Right now I'd like to tear off my shirt, run
out on the beach before it's gone past half-tide
and sieve up a couple quarts of coquinas
those minuscule molluscs that bubble up
like a splintered rainbow embedded in the sand.

Then I'd stew them a spell in rain barrel water
to brew a Florida seashore broth
wild and steamy as porpoise breath.
Sipping that with a chunk of hot cornbread
I'd take an amble back into her book
just as if out walking for pleasure
and follow her trail of crushed oyster shells,
a revelation to walk on barefoot,
the sun lifting a scent from the shells
like the vanishing smell of a hooked fish let go.

25 (Autumn 1996)

ALISON BRACKENBURY

Calf Sound

You heard the seal upon its rock
Neither fish nor deer
Black and glossy, silk of sea
Its cry rose clear

A lilting voice, a keening
The wind ran in that call
The white song that a bone blew
The love in it would kill.

You will not be a kind mother
Or faithful to your kin
If you stay on the cropped green turf.
Come in. Come in.

The hut has clouded windows
Kettles, dry plates, strong tea.
Your black eyes swim with moon's light
The dripping track to sea.

34 (Autumn 1999)

KWAME DAWES

Hawk

for Rosalie Richardson

Old Mama talked with her fingers;
sipped her liquor till time stopped.

Old Mama smiled rueful days,
whispered her secrets always

to the faithful wind, always going
some place, coming back forgetful

every time, of whose lips it had kissed,
whose secrets tasted at midnights.

We have lost Mama to the wind,
she left clothes, shoes, pills

and a bag of funky stories behind,
buried in her underthings, her hair-pins.

Putting her away, smelling her presence
we break into songs – weaving her sentences

together, like the clumpy plaits she made
of our hair in the soft of kerosene light.

At the grave-side, we stare at the swoop
of predator jets, circling the Base,

and Maude walks with Mama's limp,
favouring her right ankle, like Mama did,

muttering 'bout the way it twisted when she ran
from the snort of a white stallion

on that slate gray Carolina dawn
when the cotton fields were blanched,

and the wind was passing by, quiet-quiet,
the diving hawks still screaming.

26 (Spring 1997)

TAMAR YOSELOFF

Biology

The first incision was the worst, the way
my scalpel sank into the strange grey flesh,
the stench, the pig's eyes shut tight,
as if he couldn't face the indignity,
his vital organs exposed. Mr. Ormanati bent over
my pig, so close I could smell mints on his breath,
trace the mound of his humpback through
his brown polyester jacket. I longed to touch it,
to see inside his refrigerator, where he kept
his insects: *cold they are easier to dissect.*
Sometimes he left the closet door ajar
and if I craned my neck I could just see
his foetal deer, asleep in its huge glass jar.

Each night I'd drag the textbook to my room,
stare at diagrams of musculature until my mother
said goodnight, then by flashlight I'd find
my dog-eared Havelock Ellis, real life stories
of every kind of fetish: shoe sniffing, grown men
in diapers, animals, paedophiles, necrophilia.
By day I'd study the postman or the butcher
hoping they'd betray some hidden desire,
or the boy in my class who sometimes stared back
when Mr. Ormanati touched the curve of the female
reproductive system with his pointer, pronounced
fallopian softly, like the name of a song.

30 (Summer 1998)

KEN SMITH

Narrow Road, Deep North

From the northbound train
white flecks on the brown ploughland
like flakes of fine snow –

they are birds, gulls,
suddenly flying. Across
winter fields somehow

I missed the white horse
on the hill that was boyhood,
all of it gone now.

Playing fields some place
that was some place once, goal posts
moved and again moved.

I'm on the run, hours,
days of the one bitter thought
on the narrow road

to my life's deep north,
in my pocket a ticket:
ADULT. ADMIT ONE.

Ah this long rocking
as the landscape turns to frost
lulling me to sleep,

weeping and weeping
over the north, for my dead,
for all my lost ones,

they who will not come
my way again, them we won't
see again, ever.

The dry northern air,
the wind will sort it all out,
and the rain, the rain.

And everywhere birds
in a glitter of flying
the landscape dancing.

At Culloden larks
that are dust in the tall air,
black flags of the crows.

Barefoot some, kilted,
charging through juniper, thorns
thistles, their faces

set to the wind, sleet,
shrapnel, grapeshot, bayonets
Cumberland's well trained

Hessian butchers –
hungry and downhearted, fell
all the wild flowers

of Scotland. Exeunt
clansmen, croftsmen, fishermen.
Bonnie Prince Dickhead,

says Billy, days away
on Skye, in the old mates' club,
and a dram to go.

Ah, water. The sunset
a riot. The far islands
where clouds are mountains

under deep white snow,
and the Hebridean *yes*
begins *no, no, no,*

and *no* again *no*
till the *yes* of it at the
sentence's finish:

aye a wee dram then.

This is for you, Jim,
whose garden is the battlefield.
This is for you, Con,

that you stay upright
and vertical in Tarbert,
this god forsaken

hole. That the Wee Free
tether the goat, the rooster,
that the seventh day

is all cold meat, is
fact friend, *in the Good Black Book
you will find mention*

*of boats: but never
a bicycle*. Things the heart
will no longer hold,

and bursts with, thoughts
on the waves and the west wind,
the long birds overhead,

heron, Brent Goose, swan,
their distant migrations,
continents their shores.

The light off the cliffs
climbing out of the dull sea
into rainclouds.

The best monuments
belong to the defeated,
and always anyway

and after a while
all the bartenders look alike
and your man goes off

the rails, *refreshments*
sounds in his ear like *fresh mints*
and on the rolling

bar on the rocking
boat asking for chewing gum
tuna's what he hears.

Let the light bleed out.
Let there be me and the landscape
and the moon, dreamer

when the dream goes out
into the next and the next,
following the tongue,

the eye, lone white house
on the hilltop, why don't I
live there?

I ran away to
Scotland, the people there to
see, and found a pound

was as round and soon
spent, home again home again
jiggety-jig.

Ah but the cold clean
air of the mountains, water,
Callanish sunlight.

And again gulls' cries,
tern, bittern, the heart's last blips
on the monitor.

Time to go home.

Then the yellow bar
comes down and the town bell rings
two, two. From the dock

a woman calls her farewells
to her man and a voice shouts
Kenny, Kenny, but

it ain't me Sunshine,
we roll in the water's heave
on *The Isle of Mull*,

on passage, the land
fading to mist and distance
on the dark water

black snouts of dolphins,
up from their own deep places
breathing in ours.

29 (Spring 1998)

PASCALE PETIT

Mirador

When Gran fell downstairs and died I wanted to visit her house,
stand on top of the stairs and at the bottom
and on each step between her life and death.
I climbed carefully as once I'd climbed through cloud forest
over the tangle of roots on my way to see
Angel Falls from the mirador of Alexander Laime.

When I reached the lookout point where the whole cataract
can be viewed, sweat in my eyes and needle-fine spray,
there was drizzle, a driving wind,
dark clouds obscured the head of the falls.
For about a third of a mile up the amphitheatre
I saw how water after it has fallen so far
seems to flow back up then fall again
as air – spirals, comets, flames.

I thought of Jimmy Angel, discoverer of these falls,
how, after his death, his wife Marie
had a bush pilot fly her right up to the head
where sudden cloud can cause a crash.
And against the winds she opened the cockpit window
to throw his ashes, spray burning her face.
Then Laime the hermit built his hut on Rat Island
so he could watch dawn turn the plummeting waters to fire.

All night Gran was restless as rockets exploded
and fireworks lit up her uncurtained windows.
By four a.m. the ninety years of her life gathered forces
against the torrent that battered the panes.
Nine hundred metres to fall from the summit.
Bone and water, bone and air, the corridors
in sandstone where marrow has carved passages,
the base so strewn with rocks I could not see the plunge-pool.

But when I went and stood in Gran's hall, looking up
at the air that contained aftershocks and echoes,
the air I wanted to collect in boxes and label,
as I'd scooped the red soil at the foot of the falls
for proof of my visit, it was as if I was underwater,
all my childhood in her house falling on my head,
against my eyes, down my mouth, all the water and fire of my life.

31 (Autumn 1998)

LES MURRAY

The Ice Indigene

Prone on its wrists, beige Bear
chins the ice, its shoulders a roll bar.
Its grand wheel-arch hindquarters

are flexed to propel this fur car
at you in a gallop
               or bouncing in a lope
after oil seals who die for you.

Snow-mortared intelligent loner,
dope-eyed, with hair in his fur.
Abhor his sleeves upraised in preaching!

Arctos can drive on water
or canter the tilting platforms
amassed on the dome of ocean.

On the whitening blue-white, where landmarks
aren't made of land, and vanish,
she can live without help.

She wakes to motherhood. Gaffs
tip her gloves. Her diet is
all meat, with guts for vegetables.

She can wrest a red whale off Inuit,
appal their harpoons,
               leave them Nunuvut.

Berg drifted to a grass shore, she'd
raven on Norsemen, those poetic terse men.
Caught flatfooted, the snowdrift garbageman

may totter cavern-voiced,
tall as tractor cabins
in the aurora's scope light,

then hibernate between divorcing
continents, in a helicopter sling.
He can be simple anywhere he's going.

33 (Summer 1999)

AUGUST KLEINZAHLER

The Tree

Pinch a branch to see if it's quick
or else the thing'll just stand
for who knows how long
sun, wind, frost, chafing it, dogs
pissing at the base
birds nesting up high where leaves had been

while years blur
and the town next door's evacuated
so the kids don't turn stupid
from the water that solvents leached into
or testicle cancer
diagnosed in the Mayor on down

Cape Canaveral is renamed Eric Dolphy
your friends all swell, turn
ugly then drop
after their cute little girls grow up to fuck brutes
marry them then breed

but that shield of bark
photons roam the grain of
and pathogens try to corkscrew into
only to fall apart and dry...

because it would not bloom
because it would not die

the axman came

35 (Spring 2000)

JEAN SPRACKLAND

The Light Collector

He knows broad daylight inside out,
can't get excited any more by the tawdry brilliance of it,
flattening everything, dumbing it down.
From an open window on the seventh floor
he watches the street scudding below, and thinks
I must make something of my life, as if it were
a bag of rags for recycling.
                              Gauzy scraps of dawn
have begun to bore him. He leans out
into the caramel light of late summer evening
smattering wet roofs and TV aerials: too rich, too obvious.

At night he daydreams tricks so bright
he feels they lend him context.
He knows he has a steady way with starlight,
can pick it up like sand on a fingertip.
He goes out under the moon, in the fabulous air
tasting of electricity. He lingers by houses with drawn curtains,
presses himself thin as a shadow and watches light
bleeding from the open doorway of a pub.
But it leaves him hungry. What he seeks
for his own broken purpose is smaller
more secretive sources: the bits you find
in the sweepings of a long day alone.
The cryptic blue cast by a computer. The smash-and-grab
of camera flash. The blade of light under the door
with voices glinting behind it.

He wants to stop all the draughts in this place
with light, he wants it to shed meaning.
In the dark kitchen he opens the fridge
and the light is so sweet and precise it leaves him aching.

36 (Summer 2000)

MARTHA KAPOS

The Wild Duck in the Attic

When our minds have shut their doors
the rooms hum as if the house,
eyes closed, rests sideways

on a pillow dreaming, each chink
half-open like a mouth.
Dreamer, we thought we knew your body

like an alphabet we'd learned by heart:
the dark wedged places
like blood under a thumbnail,

a crescent of shadow
in the fold of a cupboard,
the skeletal elbow of the stairs bending,

your skin so transparent it's like
two inches of tap water in the bath.
But now all that matters is the light –

the sharp slit under the attic door
rushing forward, thin white arms open
wide enough to hold an auditorium,

while we, suspending disbelief,
sink down in our seats to watch
the house begin to swing

around its mooring like a boat.
In the shifting wind
the attic door blows open like a shining example.

And now we're seeing that other place
twilit as the underside of the sea.
We're seeing where the wild duck lies

the colour of water hiding at the bottom,
in a new kind of drowning.
Nothing is less certain than this

vast handkerchief of ocean rumpled
by the wind, this low miniature sky
the wild duck dabbling her orange feet,

looping her neck in thought under her wing.
Breathe your secret breath, wild duck,
like a god in the dark.

40 (Autumn 2001)

SAVIANA STANESCU

The Infanta Isabella

on a Saturday night they walled up
isabella under the warm glow
of candelabras holding fingers not
candles fingers burning as punishment
because she reached out with her hands
for a forbidden fruit: a red leather hat
the last word in hats shame on her
a hat in the shape of a bell
how could an infanta wear a whore's
hat a cloche that grew only God knows how
on an age-old tree at the castle
chop down all the trees they bear strange fruit
damn their seeds! who planted them?
burn the garden poison the gardener
the keeper of the garden where isabella reached out
with her fingers for a forbidden thought
nobody could save her she was walled up
inside a hoopskirt two meters by two meters
gradually she turned as hard as stone and became
the clapper of a bell ISABELLLLAAAAAA

they hung her in the chapel
high above the castle

Translated from the Romanian by
Adam J. Sorkin and Aura Sibisan
40 (Autumn 2001)

GREG DELANTY

On Reading the Diaries of Christopher Columbus

The weather's like April in Andalucía, with zephyrs,
          and the mornings are a delight.
Thus wrote Don Christóbal, and so say I, having come
          down from my book-walled crow's nest
to the stern deck overlooking the lake-calm water.
          The un-raked grass
of our garden turns from green to gold.
          So much of today
becomes so much of that day, everything
          becoming everything.
A brown-headed, red bodied damselfly settles on
          our transom
before taking off. She zips open space,
          the damselpoetry herself,
winging it back and forth from place and time, now
          to this geezer,
then back to Don Christóbal Colon on this Friday
          the thirteenth, lucky as any day,
to inform him he might have stayed at home, that the booty
          is hereandhereandhere,
the mirabilia of the Now World. Look, how the bluebottle
          who yesterday was wingèd disease,
has turned into a blue-green gem glimmering on my page,
          straight off today's diadem.

41 (Spring 2002)

STANLEY MOSS

Babies

Babies, babies,
before you can see more than light or darkness,
before your mothers have kissed your heads,
I come to you with news of dead and dying friends.
You so close to the miracle of life,
lend me a miracle to bring to my friend.
Babies, babies.
Once Death was a baby, he grasped God's little finger
to keep from falling – kicking and chortling
on his back, unbaptized, uncircumcised,
but invited to share sunlight and darkness
with the rest of us. Mother Death would nurse him,
comfort and wash him when he soiled himself
in the arms of the mourners and the heartbroken.

Older, Death took his place
at table beside his mother – her 'angel'.
They ate and drank from each other's mouth and fingers,
laughed at their private jokes. He could play
any musical instrument, knew all music by heart,
all birdsong, the purr, growl, snort, or whine
of each and every animal.
The story goes that, fat with eternal life,
older than his mother, he devoured her,
far from light or darkness.

Babies, at the moment of your first uncertain breath,
when your mother's magic blood is still upon you,
I come to you, the helpless ones still coughing
from miracles of birth.
Babies hardly heavier than clouds,
in desperation, for my friend, for a lark
I hold up the sac you broke through
as if it were Saint Veronica's Veil –
but no face is on it, no blood.
I hope up a heavy sack of useless words.
I shake a rattle to catch your eye or first smile.

41 (Spring 2002)

IAN DUHIG

Blood

Tip-toed to flex brand new Squire Shop ox blood Oxfords,
Their Chippendale varnish palimpsests of spit and polish
Finished with one occult pass from the black shoe brush
To Rembrandt a veneer even now reflecting veal-pale calves,
White Orlon ankle socks beneath petrol blue Levi Sta-Prest,
Their baked creases rising to the occasion of red braces,
Clip-ons, a half-inch in width, over brick red and duck egg
Brunswick triple-stripe button-down collared Ben Sherman,
Rizla packet- and packet-of-three-shaped bulges in its pocket,
Then up to plenty more 14-year-old slunk-vellum neck,
Bum fluff, stench of Brut, No6s, cod and chips, light and bitter,
Pilot-style, gold framed, honey-tint-lensed polaroids,
Crop fuzzed from No2 skin to a chichi revisionist suedehead
Inclined to the painted window of Luke's Tattoo Parlour,
Faking diabolical temptation to turn over a new leaf of
Your as-yet-still-virginal unilluminated manuscript
For a Yakuza body-suit, blood eagle, bull's head, Celtic snake,
Web, dragon, axe, scrolled heart, skull, drum or trumpet,
Knowing them eraseable only by Goldfinger's laser beam
When last Wednesday outside the School Nurse's office,
In front of the whole queue of third years, you blacked out
Simply from glimpsing her lance of a vaccination needle.

41 (Spring 2002)

TOMAŽ ŠALAMUN

Nations

Nations who stop telling their story
die. Scented with oil, they are the direct
access to the heart of the world.
They don't feel like making circles
or running barefoot in the snow, anymore.
Nations who stop telling their story
do not tremble under the weight
of incomprehensible powers, they
themselves are the stars
that are before them, they
themselves become stars,
the nations who live in grace and luxury.
They wake up to a handsome young

Arab who lies on the left side of them.
While he dances and talks they make
love to him, morning and evening.
They spread their almighty tent over him,
the nations who stop
telling their story.
The nations who stop telling their
story are simply wiped out by
lust, their elegant and unimportant
life is of interest only to the knife
of the horsemen, the buddies who sent
Hassan.

Translated from the Slovenian by
Phillis Levin and the author
43 (Autumn 2002)

JANE DRAYCOTT

The Tor

Coming down she met the others coming up,
moving together like eggs in a basket
or thoughts she'd had while walking home from school.

They looked like total strangers now, pale and grey.
She wondered if that was how she'd looked: climbing
through cloud to what they imagined must be sun.

She wanted to tell them how at the summit
it was raining, snowing, too windy to stand,
that all she desired now was to walk back home
the way she'd come and read about them by the fire

but none of them was listening – together
they stared ahead to the top, the strange tower
whose purpose no-one knew, and hidden from view
what might have been lightning, flashing, turning, blue.

44 (Spring 2003)

JOHN KINSELLA

Chainsaw

The seared flesh of wood, cut
to a polish, deceives: the rip and tear
of the chain, its rapid cycling
a covering up of raw savagery.
It is not just machine. In the blur
of its action, in its guttural roar,
it hides the malice of organics.
Cybernetic, empirical, absolutist.
The separation of Church and State,
conspiracies against the environmental
lobby, enforcement of fear, are at the core
of its modus operandi. The cut of softwood
is deceptive, hardwood dramatic: just
before dark on a chill evening
the sparks rain out – dirty wood,
hollowed by termites, their digested

sand deposits, capillaried highways
imploded: the chainsaw effect.
It is not subtle. It is not ambient.
It is trans nothing. A clogged airfilter
has it sucking up more juice –
it gargles, floods, chokes
into silence. Sawdust dresses boots,
jeans, the field. Gradually
the paddock is cleared, the wood
stacked in cords along the lounge-room wall.
A darkness kicks back and the cutout
bar jerks into place, a distant chainsaw
dissipates. Further on, some seconds later,
another does the same. They follow
the onset of darkness, a relay of severing,
a ragged harmonics stretching back
to its beginning – gung-ho,
blazon, overconfident. Hubristic
to the final cut, last drop of fuel.

40 (Autumn 2001)

EAMON GRENNAN

Not So Still Life with Rain and Bees

Even under the rain that throws a fine white blanket over the mountain and the lake
And smothers the green islands and soaks the grass and makes a solid slow dripping
Trickle in the sycamore; even under the rain that's general all over the valley and beyond;
Even under the steady rain measuring my life here on my perch beside the big window;
Even under the remorseless singleminded grinding and colonising hegemony of rain

The bees are out there among the furled or open flapping skirts of the fuchsia bells,
Drifting till they find a fresh one, then settling and entering, gathering what they need
In a slow deliberate shuddering of their whole body shaking suddenly the honey-core
And then extracting themselves in silence – a little heavier, their thighs gilded with pollen –

To go on cruising under the dust-fine deliquescence of damp that is the falling rain.

45 (Summer 2003)

D. NURKSE

The Evacuation Corridor

1

When I strolled up from the subway
it was raining bits of paper –
a commuter beside me
unfurled his black umbrella –
but I noticed the margins were singed.
A gilt-framed photo landed at my feet
and raised a cloud. Was I walking in dust?

I bent and licked my finger
and cleaned the faces – a mother and child
blurred by soot, beaming at me.
Could I leave them?

I had no right to that happiness
and the bronze scallops were searing.
Stamped on the back was the word RUTH.

A voice behind me shouted *hurry*
and another screamed *mercy*.
I braced my shoulders.
All around me were voices
pushing, pushing like men,
and men crying like children,
and a child calling *help*
from behind a pebbled glass door.

The island had been sealed.

2

A policeman said:
*if you breathe that cloud
you will die* as if suggesting
some other escape:

but we did not walk faster
or falter; there was a rhythm
we were obeying, just under the limit
of the weakest in the crowd,
and for years after,
perhaps until the last day,
we would be faithful to it.

The haze united us
and the wrinkles on our faces
became outlined as in greasepaint
in that red dust
in which there was no joy or sorrow,
no word for joy or sorrow –

so we left our city, and the cloud settled
on the far shore and the people in it
also held each other, tenderly, absently,
and had no need of names.

45 (Summer 2003)

YANG LIAN

Concentric Circles: Chapter One

1

fear of cold left behind by the cold
pale height of rocks left behind by blindness of rocks
ear-piercing autumn   by atrophied trees
subtracted through the trunk

then wind   not among withered branches but human bones only
not fruit skin but decayed hearing only
not to polish wings but to polish the ages-old chorus of metals only

the dead project themselves through dense fog   leaving death behind
empty fields   dark vision where furrows emit the smell of stew
frozen stiff walnuts twisted off one by one
among addresses of wine by the glass   a bright sea cold and grim
every minute empties out a cathedral where our fears are kept

subtracted   to the sum of destruction

2

there is always what's heard vaguely in a dim corridor
buzzing in the ears   moves from far away outside the ears

above a stony sea-level
sound   breaking up the chord of bird bone
chases in reverse a body that can feel pain
our bodies born again and again by a pair of pink organs

reality always intensified   tunnel blowing a gale
a thousand cacti married to a composer's night shade
from high above goats' empty orbits exceed our air

sound moves away from ears   is smashed to pieces

3

fear   between valley and valley the hydatiform mole
fear   between gold and gold
                                        ruins of man
pipe organ shine   wades across the river pissed by a bedwetting baby
sunshine   lifelong silence dropped by a cloud
                                        what's heard
always kneads the flame of pubic hair between sleeps
between days   a stomach has night-sweats in the midnight sky
silence   opens the dark score of granite

fear our fearlessness   between mountain road and mountain road
sharp reeds of bird have no fear of scratching the morning with
sit   fear no chair
got to rely on white bones sticking out of fingertips
                                        pay attention to the show
old women's weeping guts dazzlingly bright
face carved into inscription   the more you listen the more it's like your own
blood resonating in a wax rainstorm
                                                    old women's weary knees
stick close   thrashing   countless dull red inflamed knees
choir   kneels on a glass rose with no fear
allow brown tongues to lick away the dew
fear no shame   so do your best to reproduce

we who are reproduced by fear   build a mountain peak
                              be heard by what can never hear and
become   the tenderest between ghost and ghost
between talking and talking white snow brilliant in four seasons
exposes a body the absolute zero of linguistics
                                        confirmed by deathly pale flaws
between blue wrinkled wombs   a distance that cannot be filled

Translated from the Chinese by
Brian Holton and Agnes Hung-Chong Chan
44 (Spring 2003)

YUSEF KOMUNYAKAA

Astrea's Footnotes

After spying at Antwerp
    for Charles II, Aphra Behn
        sang of tropic Surinam

over winter stones for warmth
    in a debtors' prison. But
        this wasn't where Oroonoko

first rolled off the tongue
    as if she'd rehearsed it
        for years in her spleen.

The tale, a faction, a lyric
    saga in a pale throat –
        a woman who pawned her rings

& dared to endow a black man
    with nobility & gallantry
        in a thicket of thieves

& scallywags. The gallery
    of voices called, 'Sappho
        famous for her gout

& guilt'. She gave her hero
    a mind. Did someone think
        that next she'd whisper

'fabulous Priapus'
    as she penned his name?
        Drops of rain throbbed

on a lily. They pranced
    out second-hand effigies
        of harlot & sluggard

to diminish her talent
    & wit beneath footprints.
        Because this daughter

of a barber & a wet nurse
    could not heal herself
        with gifts of Indian

feathers & butterflies,
    but with only flesh itself,
        she was a satirist's envoi:

'Poverty, poetry, pox,
    are plagues enough for one.'
        Those louts tried to steal

her image & whittle it
    down to a mutable footnote,
        to a blade of lye soap

they bathed with till
    it was a sliver of regret,
        not even half as noble

as Oroonoko, who stood
    in a forest to behead
        his beloved & cover her with petals.

45 (Summer 2003)

SHARON OLDS

Satin Maroon

In the narrow office on Shattuck and Ashby,
the woman pulled open a file drawer,
low tumble of wheels on rails,
and took out the ashes, in a satin maroon
plastic box, and set them on the desk.
Next of kin, I signed, and lifted them
up, and in the car I clasped her
tight, my arms seemed encircled around
the container twice, three times. Then I held her
up to my ear, and tilted her,
to hear whatever I could hear of her,
shirr of wisdom-teeth, of kiln bed
grit, dry mince like the crab-claws that she would
shuck to give us the brine-meat – gravel
rustle. The minister opened the chapel,
we set her where she'd always sat,
we put a rose beside her like
a petticoat. Then there she was,
on the sequoia pew, a magenta carton of
mortar-and-pestled bones. That it should
come to this. I kissed the smooth
surface, under which her silver
constellations turned, and then it was
time to leave her, overnight,
as we had planned, but it was hard to leave her
by herself, but suddenly, I saw
she had always been alone – fatherless,
mismothered – and not without her own
valiant spirit. And I wished she could descant
all night, as if this were she, this rattle of
salty campfire rubble from inside her,
and I left her there, I relinquished her
to the strangeness, the still home, of matter.

46 (Autumn 2003)

MARK DOTY

In Their Flight

Who believes in them?

It doesn't matter much
to the souls, newly set free,
wheeling in the air over the site

of their last engagements.
Suppose we could see them?
They'd be like sparrows – not *like*,

they'd *be* birds, one of those autumn flocks

when the solitaries gather in great numbers,
over the waste places and the remaining fields,
turning in the air as if together they made a huge piece of cloth

folding in on itself, or a mathematical diagram of folding...
No hurry, nothing obscuring the air for them –
vast sky, entirely light-washed,

as they assemble into a great progression of pattern.
In community at last, we want to proceed in our flock, our troop...

*

Incorporated into a radiant vitality without ceasing...

You want more than that?

Of course you do: you want the steady
mosquito-drone to go on and on, ceaselessly,

you want to be the one who gets to do the perceiving
forever, of course you do.

*

But here's my guess:

it's another thing for the dead;
they've been singular long enough.

We can't let ourselves see what
enormous work it is
to be one of something, to exert
the will to sustain those boundaries.
The dead, rimless,

loosed from particularity,
move out toward the edge of the city,
someplace the flock can unknot itself

freely, where they can feast in the fields
oblivious to the column of smoke roiling behind them.

*

Anniversary day, evil wind banging the door to the gym
till the glass shattered, and Mauricio said,
– in a low voice, as if to say it would somehow protect him –

Lot of spirits blowing around today.

48 (Summer 2004)

SINÉAD MORRISSEY

The Second Lesson of the Anatomists

See how the inside belies our skin,
say the anatomists,
after showing us how freakishly we split;

the outside smooth and assiduous
unto itself, while the inside
baffles and seethes.

The lung-wonder held over the heart-wonder
and the heart-wonder bleeding, emptying, re-bleeding,
and spit, in different colours, oiling their hands.

Are all skins as effortlessly deceptive as this?
The thin film over the ocean? Doors?
Or this evening, for instance,

in which darkness and a river
play both mother and father
in supporting a glass room?

There is a party going on. There is wine
and a light fixture being obedient
unto itself. And then there is this spillage

in the centre
from somewhere stranger and more extravagant
which has drawn us all here.

I think of the second lesson of the anatomists.
I think of eggshells cracking open
from the inside.

For we have hallways to discover in one another like nerves.
And childhoods, and love affairs, and drownings, and faithfulness
by which language has occurred.

44 (Spring 2003)

KATHERINE PIERPOINT

Buffalo Calf

A buffalo calf, beautiful, lies asleep under the water-tap.
A calf, bright oil-drum black, blissful, at hot roost,
front legs folded in the shitty mud,
and eyes rolled back,
smiling hugely –
he's a deformed fairy,
or drugged, ecstatic dragon, landed half-on, half-in the earth.

Dripped on,
he sucks, eyes shut, all day, on that one sensation.

A slow, kohl-eyed cow walks by, to her daily fieldwork in the rice,
but dressed in the tassels, paint, and tin bells of a dancer –
she's made more beautiful each moment through her movement.

A temple elephant too. The surprise of it – in town! at church! –
for an elephant is its own cathedral.
Even thinking of an elephant
is architecture, elaborate; a plain hugeness at first disguising the subtleties there;
and there it stands and stands, and stands, at the busy temple gate,
little as a lap-dog
against the mounting pyramid of stones,
the mass of carvings, the unending, up-ending sex,
the linked aeons of miracles.

Polka-dot flowers and river deltas chalked across her steep forehead,
as if bringing out her private depths and cliffs of thought,
the bright hibiscus in there, the mudfields, long bathes;
and she sways, bored, bored, bored,
leaning this way and that against the air.

48 (Summer 2004)

PETER REDGROVE

Who Is the Higher Penis Here?

I was visiting
      the Mother of Wolves
            in her firelit cave,
Her sons and daughters tugging
      and wrestling around,
            but the higher penis
Today, was a quietly spoken
      Victorian scientist
            practising spiritualism
With only three ghosts,
      he took me elsewhere, to
            Dr. Jekyll's laboratory
Where intercourse was not only
      imminent but eminent too,
            and immanent: the cave
Just would not do;
      and I felt an invisible flow up
            and around my high penis
And the Lady Doctor felt it too,
      it was like the pressure of light,
            like the chamber
Of a goldleaf electroscope,
      crura of the charged instrument
            parting legs;
Science was OK as a direct allegory
      of the lower penis, rising;
            the psychic penis rolling
Clouds of the seminal ectoplasm
      risen for consultation,
            this was high colloquy
But it was still penis, stiff sage,
      winking to his two companions, whispering
            of doorlocks
Oily with harmonious toil, true science;
      practising spiritualism
            with only one ghost.

49 (Autumn 2004)

DALJIT NAGRA

Darling & Me

Di barman's bell done dinging
      so I phone di dimply mississ,
Putting some gas on cookah,
      bonus pay I bringin!

Downing drink, I giddily
      home for Pakeezah record
to which we go-go, tango,
      for roti – to kitchen – she rumba!

I tell her of poor Jimmy John,
      in apron his girlfriend
she bring to pub his plate of
      chicken pie and dry white

potato! Like Hilda Ogden,
      Heeya, eaht yor chuffy dinnaaah!
She huffing off di stage
      as he tinkle his glass of Guinness.

We say we could never eat
      in publicity like dat, if we did
wife advertisement may need
      of solo punch in di smack.

I pull her to me – my skating
      hands on her back are Bolero
by Torvill and Dean. Giggling
      with bhangra arms in air

she falling for lino, till I
      swing her up in forearm!
Darling is so pirouettey with us
      for whirlwind married month,

that every night, though by day
      we work factory-hard, she always
have disco of drumstick in pot.
      Hot. Waiting for me.

Pakeezah – soundtrack to the
Bollywood film of the same name
Roti – Punjabi proverbial for dinner

49 (Autumn 2004)

MATTHEW HOLLIS

Isostasy

Isostasy n. Equilibrium or stability due to equality of
(hydrostatic) pressure

And another thing I didn't say:
that the upward mass of a cresting wave
will always momentarily equate
to the average human being's weight;
so that if your timing is exact,
your footfall strict, and you've cracked
the basic rudiments of fetch,
you can run across the sea from one edge
to another on a causeway made
of temporality and water. Please mind
to keep that close next time the scale
has got too broad to broach, the pale
well passed beyond; and come down then
against your coast to hear the sound of feet
run in across the rooftops of the sea.
This much is truth, in principle at least.

47 (Spring 2004)

RAÚL ZURITA

from INRI

The Sea

Amazing harvests rained out of the sky. Incredible ripe fruit onto the ploughed fields of the sea. Viviana hears mute silhouettes fall, minutes that did not finish, sacred crosses that rain like clouds onto the waves of the Pacific. She hears torsos, strange mists coming off the waves, strange clouds of soft flesh against the empty sky of the ocean.

Baits rain down with mouthless angels, with scores that could not be heard, with soundless shadows that kiss. Amazing harvests rain down, fall down, extraordinary trees that fall burning into the waves.

Ploughed fields, sacred lands rain from the sky with broken backs, pieces of necks that weren't there any more, unexpected clouds of unending spring. They were thrown. They rain down. Amazing harvests of men come down as food for the fish in the sea. Viviana hears sacred lands rain down, hears her son fall like a cloud onto the unclouded cross of the Pacific.

*

Crosses made of fish for the Christs. The arch of the Chilean sky falls on the bloody tombs of Christ for the fishes. That's your mother, there. That's your son. Shadows fall on the sea. Strange human baits fall on the crosses of fish in the sea. Viviana wants to cradle fishes in her arms, wants to hear that clear day, that love cut short, that fixed sky. Viviana is now Chile. She cradles fish under the sky that shouts hosanna.

Surprising Christs fall in strange positions onto the crosses of the sea. Surprising baits rain from the sky: a last prayer rains, a last passion, a last day under the sky's hosannas. Infinite skies fall in strange positions onto the sea.

Infinite skies fall, infinite skies of broken legs, of arms bent against the neck, of heads wrenched against backs. Skies weep downwards falling in broken poses, in clouds of broken backs and broken skies. They fall, they sing.

That's your mother, there. That's your son.

*

That's your son. Viviana hears the arches of eyebrows incredibly raised, hears eyes endlessly open falling from the sky's eyebrows. Hears the nails sinking into the cross of the ocean. The whole Chilean sea is the cross. Infinite plains sing from the sky the hosanna of the cross which is the sea, of the food which falls like plains, like pieces of bread into the sacred stomach of the fish. Viviana hears infinite sacred shoals emerging, infinite fish singing with a voice taken from the sky.

The fish go up into the sky. Surprising baits rained down with surprising days, with images of almond trees, with loves cut short. Surprising baits rained on the sacred sea, on the sacred fish.

The sea is holy, holy the wide plains of human fruits that fall, the fish holy. I heard infinite days falling, bodies that fell with skies, with fields glimpsed between them, with trees like a chorus of crosses that sang out in songsung waters. Viviana cradles the holy sea. Viviana says somewhere in these sacred waters is her son.

*

Holy skies rained down. Infinities of water like sons of the holy sky, yes, like pieces of bread, like holy baits beneath the ocean cross of Chile. They wept, rained down sons of loves that never more, of endless meadows that fell in flames, of bushes that burn and do not burn up. Viviana hears whole skies fall like almond trees in flower, like pink cheeks in flower on the redeemed sea of Chile.

The bush that is the Chilean sea burns and does not burn up.

The holy plains of the sky burn falling. Human baits fall onto the flaming bush of the ocean. The fish swim up singing with the voice of the sky, shoals, infinities of fish rise up from the sacred waters.

Strange suns sing raining from the sky, strange fruits on the sacred ocean.

Fish in flames leap, amazing baits burn in the sea. Holy skies rained. Bushes of Chile, there are your sons. Bushes of Chile, there is the sea in flames.

Translated from the Spanish by William Rowe
50 (Spring 2005)

ELAINE FEINSTEIN

A Visit

I still remember love like another country
      with an almost forgotten landscape
of salty skin and a dry mouth. I think
      there was always a temptation to escape
from the violence of that sun, the sudden
      insignificance of ambition,
the prowl of jealousy like a witch's cat.

Last night I was sailing in my sleep
      like an old seafarer, with scurvy
colouring my thoughts, there was moonlight
      and ice on green waters.
Hallucinations. Dangerous nostalgia.
      And early this morning you whispered
as if you were lying softly at my side:

'Are you still angry with me?' And spoke my
      name with so much tenderness, I cried.
I never reproached you much
      that I remember, not even when I should;
to me, you were the boy in Ravel's garden
      who always longed to be good,
as the forest creatures knew, and so do I.

46 (Autumn 2003)

MARILYN HACKER

Glose

And I grew up in patterned tranquility
In the cool nursery of the new century.
And the voice of man was not dear to me,
But the voice of the wind I could understand.

Anna Akhmatova, 'Willow',
translated by Judith Hemschmeyer

The sibilant wind predicted a latish spring.
Bare birches leaned and whispered over the gravel path.
Only the river ever left. Still, someone would bring
back a new sailor middy to wear in the photograph
of the four of us. Sit still, stop *whispering*.
– Like the still-leafless trees with their facility
for lyric prologue and its gossipy aftermath,
I liked to make up stories. I liked to sing;
was encouraged to cultivate that ability.
And I grew up in patterned tranquility.

In the single room, with a greasy stain like a scar
from the gas-fire's fumes, when any guest might be a threat
(and any threat was a guest – from the past or the future)
at any hour of the night, I would put the tea things out
though there were scrap-leaves of tea, but no sugar,
or a lump or two of sugar but no tea.
Two matches, a hoarded cigarette:
my day's page ashed on its bier in a bed-sitter.
No godmother had presaged such white nights to me
in the cool nursery of the young century.

The human voice distorted itself in speeches,
a rhetoric that locked locks and ticked off losses.
Our words were bare as that stand of winter birches
while poetasters sugared the party bosses'
edicts (the only sugar they could purchase)
with servile metaphor and simile.
The effects were mortal, however complex the causes.
When they beat their child beyond this thin wall, his screeches,
wails and pleas were the gibberish of history,
and the voice of man was not dear to me.

Men and women, I mean. Those high-pitched voices –
how I wanted them to shut up! They sound too much
like me. Little machines for evading choices,
little animals, selling their minds for touch.
The young widow's voice is only hers. She memorizes
the words we read and burn, nights when we read and
burn with the words unsaid, hers and mine, as we watch
and are watched, and the river reflects what spies. Is
the winter trees' rustling a code to the winter land?
But the voice of the wind I could understand.

54 (Summer 2006)

SEAMUS HEANEY

To Pablo Neruda in Tamlaghtduff

Niall Fitzduff brought a jar
of crab apple jelly
made from crabs off the tree
that grew at Duff's Corner –
still grows at Duff's Corner –
a tree I never once saw
with crab apples on it.

Contrary, unflowery
sky-whisk and bristle, more
twig-fret than fruit-fort,
crabbed
as crabbed could be –
that was the tree
I remembered.

But then –
O my Pablo of earthlife –
when I tasted the stuff
it was freshets and orbs.

My eyes were on stalks,
I was back in an old
rutted cart road, making
the rounds of the district, breasting
its foxgloves, smelling
cow-parsley and nettles, all
of high summer's smoulder
under our own tree ascendant
in Tamlaghtduff,
its crab-hoard and – yes,
in pure hindsight – corona
of gold.
              For now,
O my home-truth Neruda,
round-faced as the crowd
at the crossroads, with your eyes
I see it, now taste-bud
and tear-duct melt down
and I spread the jelly on thick
as if there were no tomorrow.

52 (Autumn 2005)

CIARAN CARSON

Redoubt

If only because in another country you are free
to renegotiate yourself or what you thought you were,

I found myself this night approached by a man in a suit.
When he asked me what I was drinking I didn't demur.

French was a lingua franca. He showed me a worn photo,
wife and children smiling at us from some Polish city.

We'd already exchanged names, whatever they were. So what
did I do? I told him I was a writer, not well-known.

Me? I'm a salesman, he said, I travel in fountain pens.
He represented all the big companies like Mont Blanc.

It was the coming back-to-the-future thing in the East,
though back where I come from, he said, they'd never gone away.

But what they desired now was 'Western exclusivity'.
And what sort of thing do you write, would you like to try mine?

Even before he proffered it I knew it was a fake.
He'd filled it with fancy ink. *De l'encre violette.*

So I wrote that I was a writer of fiction and poems,
and if you're about to ask me what they're about, I said,

that's for the reader to say, whose guess is as good as mine.
He smiled. And how did it all end up? I said, picturing

the scene, bottles with strange labels glinting in the background,
the bartender pretending to polish a glass, and you

looking the Mont Blanc man in the eye. I imagined snow
outside, the footsteps that brought you there already erased

as were his that crossed yours at the threshold if not before,
as you were a stranger to me once when we first met.

I stared at my face for an age in the en suite mirror.
Then I must have crawled into bed before my mind went blank.

57 (Summer 2007)

CAROL RUMENS

Little Epic

L'anguilla, torcia, frusta,
freccia d'Amore in terra
Montale, 'L'anguilla'

Everything was yet to be imagined –
even the river with her sandy blushes,
slithering up the chrome-work barrier,
and the bridge, that heron slenderness, its soaring
cruelly earthed by strings of disguised rain;
motorways, beach-walks – vanishing perspectives
of latitude – all were unmeasured since
geography had never heard of you;
and nothing in the six-fold darkness stirred.
A god can have his project almost finished
before he lights upon that little spiral
of mud which seethes it into sense, but I,
the lesser maker, needed last things first:
before the supernovae, clouds, volcanoes
and icebergs – Adam! Stealthily engraved
(work of a star, perhaps, I dared not ask)
a human symbol lit the stone. The river
edged around it, birds hovered above it:
museums were bright with fish, shopping-malls
                            claimed the sea.
Everything was more itself since printed
with some fine trace of you; even the air
feathered uncertainly into a footprint.
Then, like the washed-up oil-drum, swamped and
                            emptied
with every thrust, I tried to turn aside
and rest – but from no angle could refuse it –
sea-fire and lash and squalor of love's earthing
till the hard shape was broken, and creation
had drained the world, leaving it bridgeless water.

54 (Summer 2006)

JACOB POLLEY

The Cheapjack

What do I have for as near as damn it?
What do I sell but I'm giving away?
   Might I pick my own pockets
   and slit my own throat
and dump myself dead in a shop doorway?

Daffodils, bird whistles, bobble hats,
fickle fish, slinkies, your name spelled in wire;
   caterpillars, mouse mats,
   trick plastic dog-shit,
conniptions, predictions and God's own fire.

I've bargained myself to Bedlam and back,
and a wonder it is that I'm not less flesh,
   for I'd sell you the scraps,
   the loose skin, the slack,
the tips of my toes and the last of my breath,

and might as well for the good my breath's done;
I've blown suits, jobs, marriages, houses and lands:
   I'm a man overcome
   by his profligate tongue,
and if you get close, you can stand where I stand.

What'll it cost? Not as much as you think.
What have you got? That'll do. Here's my nod,
   here's my wink,
   here's my blood for the ink.
I'm begging you now: my life for the lot.

53 (Spring 2006)

KATHRYN SIMMONDS

Sunday at the Skin Launderette

The weekly visit to the perfumed steam. Outside
rain falls biblically, a reminder of the duty to be clean.
Inside no one notices – they're too busy with the work
of choosing a machine, counting change and making
sure the temperature's just right, trying not to pour
the powder anywhere but in the slot. Other skin

begins revolving through the plastic portholes. Skin
of fine Thai origin, Kenyan and Jamaican skin beside
the bluish white, the tattooed, mottled and poor
stretch-marked stuff, every kind of hair licked clean.
A fat man doubles over on a bench – he's making
heavy weather of it, separating folds, trying to work

his penis from its shell. It's slow and careful work.
His lungs balloon as he un-sheathes his foreskin,
fragile as sushi, then the balls, until he's making
progress, loosening his mass of satin arse. Beside
him a girl unpeels her arm, a glove which comes clean
off revealing sinews. The man squeezes his paw,

fatty and raw, gathers his acreage while the girl pours
a gloss of layers over her hips, pausing to work
around the knees, the difficult toes. The clean
fug of detergents is dizzying as she drapes her skin
over her arm like a silk evening gown. Beside
her an old woman undresses patiently, making

sure not to tear her cobweb elbows, making
sure the birth mark is preserved. She pauses
at her clavicle and strokes the scar on the side
of her brow, puckered like a wonky zip. She works
at this delicate undoing, unpeeling the skin
which is sheer as moth wing now, until her lean

frame hangs with crushed silk, the body coming clean
at last. So they sit waiting, staring into space, making
lists in their heads, watching the machines. While his skin
tumbles dry, the man examines his heart. The women pore
over their bodies, carefully lift their breasts to work
out once again where their souls are hiding. Outside

a skin of rain ripples the darkening streets as water pours
through gutters, pounding pavements clean, making
everything a sort of new, while the work goes on inside.

55 (Autumn 2006)

COLETTE BRYCE

Self-portrait in the Dark (with Cigarette)

To sleep, perchance
to dream? No chance:
it's 4 a.m. and I'm wakeful
as an animal,
caught between your presence and the lack.
This is the realm insomniac.
On the window seat, I light a cigarette
from a slim flame, and monitor the street –
a stilled film, bathed in amber,
softened now in the wake of a downpour.

Beyond the daffodils
on Magdalen Green, there's one slow vehicle
pushing its beam along Riverside Drive,
a sign of life;
and two months on
from 'moving on'
your car, that you haven't yet picked up,
waits spattered in raindrops like bubblewrap.
Here, I could easily go off
on a riff

on how cars, like pets, look a little like their owners
but I won't 'go there'
as they say in America
given it's a clapped-out Nissan Micra…
And you don't need to know that
I've been driving it illegally at night
in the lamp-lit silence of this city
– you'd only worry –
or, worse, that Morrissey
is jammed in the tape deck now and for eternity;

no. It's fine, all gleaming hubcaps,
seats like an upright, silhouetted couple;
from the dashboard, the wink
of that small red light I think
is a built-in security system.
In a poem
it could represent a heartbeat or a pulse.
Or loneliness: its vigilance.
Or simply the lighthouse-regular spark
of someone, somewhere, smoking in the dark.

53 (Spring 2006)

ALICE OSWALD

Dunt

a poem for a nearly dried-up river

Very small and damaged and quite dry,
a Roman Waternymph made of bone
tries to summon a river out of limestone.

Very eroded faded,
her left arm missing and both legs from the knee down,
a Roman Waternymph made of bone
tries to summon a river out of limestone.

Exhausted, utterly worn down,
a Roman Waternymph made of bone,
being the last known speaker of her language,
she tries to summon a river out of limestone.

Little distant sound of dry grass. Try again.

A Roman Waternymph made of bone,
very endangered now,
in a largely unintelligible monotone,
she tries to summon a river out of limestone.

Little distant sound as of dry grass. Try again.

Exquisite bone figurine with upturned urn,
in her passionate self-esteem, she smiles, looking sideways.
She seemingly has no voice but a throat-clearing rustle
as of dry grass. Try again.

She tries leaning,
pouring pure outwardness out of a grey urn.

Little slithering sounds as of a rabbit man in full night gear.
Who lies so low in the rickety willow-herb
that a fox trots out of the woods
and over his back and away. Try again.

She tries leaning,
pouring pure outwardness out of a grey urn.
Little lapping sounds. Yes.
As of dry grass secretly drinking. Try again.

Little lapping sounds yes
as of dry grass secretly drinking. Try again.

Roman bone figurine,
year after year in a sealed glass case,
having lost the hearing of her surroundings,
she struggles to summon a river out of limestone.

Little shuffling sound as of approaching slippers.

Year after year in a sealed glass case
a Roman Waternymph made of bone,
she struggles to summon a river out of limestone.

Pause. Little shuffling sound as of a nearly dried-up woman,
not really moving through the fields,
having had the gleam taken out of her
to the point where she resembles twilight. Try again.

Little shuffling clicking.
She opens the door of the church.
Little distant sounds of shutaway singing. Try again.

Little whispering fidgeting of a shutaway congregation
wondering who to pray to.
Little patter of eyes closing. Try again.

Very small and damaged and quite dry,
a Roman Waternymph made of bone,
she pleads she pleads a river out of limestone.

Little hobbling tripping of a nearly dried-up river
not really moving through the fields,
having had the gleam taken out of it
to the point where it resembles twilight.
Little grumbling shivering last-ditch attempt at a river
more nettles than water. Try again.

Very speechless, very broken old woman
her left arm missing and both legs from the knee down,
she tries to summon a river out of limestone.

Little stoved-in sucked-thin
low-burning glint of stones
rough-sleeping and trembling and clinging to its rights.

Victim of Swindon.
Puddle midden.
Slum of overgreened foot-churn and pats
whose crayfish are cheap tool kits
made of the mud stirred up when a stone's lifted.

It's a pitiable likeness of clear running,
struggling to keep up with what's already gone:
the boat the wheel the sluice gate,
the two otters larricking along. Go on.

And they say oh they say
in the days of better rainfall
it would flood through five valleys,
there'd be cows and milking stools
washed over the garden walls
and when it froze, you could skate for five miles. Yes go on.

Little loose-end shorthand unrepresented
beautiful disused route to the sea,
fish path with nearly no fish in.

55 (Autumn 2006)

DAVID HARSENT

Spatchcock

Jean Dubuffet, *L'Arbre de fluides*;
Susan Hiller, *From the Freud Museum*

As I entered, she had her pinking shears to the backbone,
having dropped the gizzard into the kitchen bin,
and barely looked over her shoulder to see who it was

when I gave the door a little back-heel
then ferreted round in the fridge for an ice-cold Coors
before slipping up from behind to cop a feel.

Another hot day in September, and that the cause
of her half-baked look, brought on
by lying bare-assed in the garden all afternoon,

a flush coming off her, the veins so close to the skin
I could trace the flow like sap, could tongue-up the ooze
of sweat at the nape of her neck: and this the real

taste of her, like nothing before, like nothing I ever knew.
You have to go hard at it, either side of the spine,
all the time bearing down against the sinew,

then lift the long bone entire and get both hands
into the cut, knuckle to knuckle, and draw
the carcass apart, and press, till you hear the breastbone crack.

Looked at like that it's roadkill, flat on its back,
sprung ribcage, legs akimbo, red side up, and sends
a message (you might guess) about life lived in the raw.

So then it's a matter of taste: herb-butter under the slack
of the breast, perhaps, or a tart marinade,
to flatter and blend, spread thinly and rubbed well in.

She favoured the latter – that and a saltire of thin
skewers driven aslant from thigh to neck,
which might, indeed, have said something about her mood.

That done, she stripped off, gathering the oils and the balm
she'd need for however long the thing would take,
and went back to her place in the sun. It did no harm,

I suppose, to watch from an upstairs window: a hawk's-
eye-view as she lay there timing the turn
(face-up till you tingle, then flip) to brown but not burn.

The marks of the griddle, the saltire, the subtle flux...
We ate it with lima beans and picked the bones,
after which we took to bed a bottle of bright Sancerre

and I held her down as I'd held her down before,
working her hot-spots with a certain caution and care
as she told me not here... or here... but there... and *there.*

I left her flat on her back – flat out and shedding a glow,
or so I like to think, as I slipped downstairs
and lifted, from a peg-board beside the hob,

her mother's (or grandmother's) longhand note on how
to spatchcock a chicken, or guinea, or quail, or squab,
or sparrow, even, with emphasis on that 'crack';

and lifted, as well, before I lifted the latch,
myrtle, borage, dill, marjoram, tarragon, sumac
all named and tagged in a customized cardboard box.

56 (Spring 2007)

PAUL MULDOON

from The Old Country

V

Every cut was a cut to the quick
when the weasel's twist met the weasel's tooth
and Christ was somewhat impolitic
in branding as 'weasels fighting in a hole', forsooth,

the petrol-smugglers back on the old sod
when a vendor of red diesel
for whom every rod was a green rod
reminded one and all that the weasel

was nowhere to be found in that same quarter.
No mere mortar could withstand a ten-inch mortar.
Every hope was a forlorn hope.

So it was that the defenders
were taken by their own blood-splendour.
Every slope was a slippery slope.

53 (Spring 2006)

CHASE TWICHELL

Savin Rock

What I know is a slur of memory,
fantasy, research, pure invention,
crime dramas, news, and witnesses
like the girl who liked to get high
and the one who was eventually
returned to her family unharmed.
The rest I made up.

The fathers drank beer in the grandstand,
flattening cans and dropping
the dull coins into the underworld.
It was daylight – we went right under,
down into the slatted dark,
the smell under the bleachers
where lots of men peed,
paper cones and dead balloons,
people jostling and whispering.
Down there were the entrances
to the dark rides, the funhouses:
Death Valley and Laff-in-the-Dark.
Of course that's not true;
they were right on the main boardwalk
under strings of bulbs lit up all night.

Mom says, *To remember something,*
go back to the place where you forgot it.
But the place was torn down
forty years ago; there are motels
there now, where the Ferris wheel
lurched up and over the trees,
over the fathers at their picnic table
close enough to feel the Tilt-a-Whirl's
crude rhythms through the ground.
They make the cars go faster or slower, depending.
After hours the boys loosen up the machines
and take girls for rides.

Hey kid! I flipped a coin in my head
and it came up tails. Want to take a walk?
He looked older than our parents.
How old did our parents look?
He was fifty, or thirty. I remember
the smell of whatever he put on his hair,
and the blue nail on his thumb.
He could flip a lit cigarette around
with his lips so the fire was inside.
I rode a little metal car
into Laff-in-the-Dark to dance
with the skeleton (possibly real
since some teeth had fillings)
that flung itself at me from the dark.

A dog watched me from a pickup window.
The World's Biggest Pig lay
beached on its side, heaving.
The tattooed lady had a tattooed baby.
No one ever tattooed a newborn child
for real, did they? The 'Chinese Dragon'
was only an iguana.

In the Maze of Mirrors
I was fatso and skeleton,
skirt blown up by a fan. Not true.
A fan blew a girl's skirt up.
It wasn't me. I was a tomboy. I wore pants.

At the stable girls in love with horses
visited and groomed and fed them daily.
For girls it was about trust,
being part of a couple,
the horse and the girl,
but for the man in the barn
it was about making girls feel
groomed and visited.
Come on over here. Didn't a guy ever
brush your hair with a currycomb?
I don't believe it! Not once?
Little honeycomb like you?
And kittens, always good bait.
A little dish of spoiled milk.

Do you think they don't pass them around?
They pass them around.
Marked kids get shared,
little pink kid tongues *lick lick licking*
like a puppy! Good dog!
And on the carousel a man appeared
from nowhere to help her on,
hand palm up on the saddle just as she sat,
squirming there until the horse pulled her away.
Little cowgirl, giddyup!

Thus she became half human half animal,
and remained so her entire life,
now a shepherdess, now a sleek young
she-goat, so lithe and small-hipped,
half tame, little goatskin haunches –
hand-fed on SnoCones and cotton candy –
the girl who was eventually
returned to her family unharmed.

Tell me, little shepherdess,
how this bodes for first love,
the centaur pissing outside your tent
in the afterlife, having come down
over the stony pastures to claim you
and feed you trout and fiddleheads
and take you to bed on the high ledges
where the wind holds you down for him.
But he won't be the first.

Sweet-sharp bouquet of darkroom,
holster with toy six-gun,
hot umbrella lamps nudged into place
by his fat pink fingers.
A little maraschino light presides over
negatives strung up like game to dry.
The tomboy's showing her rump,
hard little buttocks under the tender wrapping,
the skin. Little wonton.

57 (Summer 2007)

PASCALE PETIT

What the Water Gave Me (VI)

after Frida Kahlo

This is how it is at the end –
me lying in my bath
                                 while the waters break,
my skin glistening with amnion,
                                         streaks of starlight.

And the waters keep on breaking
as I reverse out of my body.

My life dances on the silver surface
where cacti flower.

The ceiling opens
                            and I float up on fire.

Rain pierces me like thorns. I have a steam veil.

I sit bolt upright as the sun's rays embrace me.

Water, you are a lace wedding-gown
I slip over my head, giving birth to my death.

I wear you tightly as I burn –
                              don't make me come back.

56 (Spring 2007)

PHILIP GROSS

Designs for the Water Garden

1.
      : glass stepping stones,
flat topped, level with the water,
so on mornings after, when a low
mist frosts the lake, the host walks
out towards the island where black
coffee waits; he calls the guests, o
ye of little faith, to join him.

2.
      : a rain-gazebo
with a narrow ceiling-well and a grille
in the floor, so whatever the sky sends
stands in our midst, passing through,
a slim visitor, greyish and graceful
and slightly distrait; we receive her
politely but she never stops for tea.

3.
      : a salmon treadwheel
where the fish in season thrashes up
the water-stair, bucket by bucket, each
time tripping the house-high millwheel
down a click. A noble fate. Like us,
it thrives on purpose, always getting
somewhere, never (*what now?*) done.

4.
      : a mist maze –
with aerosol-fine fountains to infuse
the walled garden with varying densities
from slight pearling to period pea-souper.
In winter, bare trees seem to pace the maze
amongst us. For the children there's always
a rainbow or two. We keep them like pets.

ALISON BRACKENBURY

5.
        : the eel scene.
Just *be* there, drive through wind and rain,
whichever night's the night. The eels are struggling
in their caged sluice. Now! We pop the bubbly,
frothing. They pour west, released into their instincts,
a slow gusher, oilily across the lawn, around
our shucked clothes in the mud, our naked feet.

6.
        : a flood-feature
like a force-field carved in silt and stuff:
the tracks of the water-beast dragging its bulk
through the garden. Its scrapings, its droppings,
twig-mats and shreddings wrapped round trees.
We contemplate it, for our own good. This is Art
and this is August and the river's miles away.

7.
        : a water-glass lens
through which you can see only water.
All the rest, dark matter… Here's the stream
through which light enters the world; there,
its tree-shaped escape to the sky; here, walking
through the night of dryness, we're revealed
as lattices of mostly water, flowing side by side.

                                58 (Autumn 2007)

Lapwings

They were everywhere. No. Just God or smoke
Is that. They were the backdrop to the road,

My parents' home, the heavy winter fields
From which they flashed and kindled and uprode

The air in dozens. I ignored them all.
'What are they?' 'Oh – peewits – ' Then a hare flowed,

Bounded the furrows. Marriage. Child. I roamed
Round other farms. I only knew them gone

When, out of a sad winter, one returned.
I heard the high mocked cry 'Pee – *wit*', so long

Cut dead. I watched it buckle from vast air
To lure hawks from its chicks. That time had gone.

Gravely, the parents bobbed their strip of stubble.
How had I let this green and purple pass?

Fringed, plumed heads (full name, the crested plover)
Fluttered. So crowned cranes stalk Kenyan grass.

Then their one child, their anxious care, came running,
Squeaked along each furrow, daft and dauntless.

Did I once know the story of their lives?
Do they migrate from Spain? Or coasts' cold run?

And I forgot their massive arcs of wing.
When their raw cries swept over, my head spun

With all the brilliance of their black and white
As though you cracked the dark and found the sun.

                                59 (Spring 2008)

ROBIN ROBERTSON

The Plague Year

Great elms gesture in the last of the light. I am dying
so slowly you'd hardly notice. What is there left
to trust but this green world and its god,
always returning to life? I stood
all day in the vanishing point; my place
now taken by a white-tailed deer.

*

I go to check the children, who are done for.
They lie there broken on their beds, limbs thrown out
in the attitudes of death, the shape of soldiers.
The next morning, I look up at my reflection
in the train window: unshaven, with today's paper;
behind me stands a gunman in a hood.

*

The chestnut trees hold out their breaking buds
like lanterns, or wounds, sticky with life. Under the
false-teeth-whistling flight of a wood-pigeon
a thrown wave of starlings rose and sank itself
back into a hedge, in a burst of chatter.
My father in the heart of the hedge, clasping a bible.

*

Rain muscles its way through the gutters
of Selma and Vine. I look north
through the fog at the Hollywood sign,
east to the observatory where tonight,
under a lack of stars,
old men will be fighting with knives.

*

Western Michigan,
on the Pere Marquette
roll-casting for steelhead:
mending my line over a drift of them
stitched into the shadows,
looking for a loophole in the water.

*

Descending a wrought-iron spiral stair, peering
down at the people very far below;
no hand-rail, every
second step rusted away, I'm holding
a suitcase and a full glass of wine,
wearing carpet slippers and a Balenciaga gown.

*

My past stretches from here to there, and back,
leaving me somewhere in the middle
of Shepherd's Bush Green with the winos of '78.
A great year; I remember it well. Hints of petrol,
urine, plane trees; a finish so long you could
sleep out under it. Same faces, different names.

*

Parrots tear out their feathers, whistling Jingle Bells,
cornfields burst into flames, rivers dry
from their source to the sea, snakes sun themselves
as the roads return to tar; puffer fish off the Lizard,
whales in the Thames, the nets heavy
with swordfish, yellowfin, basking shark.

*

Cyclamen under olive trees; sacked tombs, a ruined
moussaka, with chips. Locals on motorbikes
chew pitta bread, stare out at me like sheep,
their wayside shrines to the saints
built better than their houses; at every bend
tin memorials to the crashed dead.

Wild Flowers

I will be sober on my wedding day,
my eggs uncracked inside my creel,
my tongue sleeping in her tray.

I will lift my breast to pay
babies with their liquid meal,
I will be sober on my wedding day.

With my hands I'll part the hay,
nest inside the golden reel,
my tongue sleeping in her tray.

I'll dance with cows and cloying grey,
spin my grassy roulette wheel,
I will be sober on my wedding day.

I'll crash to muddy knees and pray,
twist the sheets in tortured zeal,
my tongue sleeping in her tray.

Church-bells shudder on the bay,
fingered winds impel the deal:
I will be sober on my wedding day,
my tongue sleeping in her tray.

58 (Autumn 2007)

---

*

I was down here in the playground
with the other adults,
on the roundabouts and swings,
while up on the hill
on the tennis court,
the children were kneeling to be shot.

*

In November, two ring-necked parakeets
eating from apples still hanging
from the apple tree. The dead crow I notice
is just a torn black bin-liner;
at the end of the garden a sand-pit stands up
as a fox, and slopes off.

*

Smoked mackerel, smoked eel, smoked halibut,
smoked reindeer heart, veal paté, six different kinds
of salmon, Gustaf's Sausage, Jansson's Temptation.
Tasting each *ex voto*, I saw the electrodes
in a bucket, the blade, the gaff, the captive bolt,
walking my plate around the stations of the dead.

60 (Summer 2008)

FRED D'AGUIAR

S-Joe

Walked the way of the road
Leading into Airy Hall
With a twist and a turn
Hither and thither in line
With plates spun by a hand
None can see but many think
Must operate rods on which
Those plates balance and shimmer
As S-Joe shimmies a few feet
Stops on a sweet spot
Reverses for almost as many
Steps and then rolls forward
Getting nowhere fast
Folk said or with all the time
Afforded those spinning
Plates tilted twice
For S-Joe in keeping
With two bends in his name
And in the road whose
Open ends admit him
Whether he shuffles backwards
Or forwards eyes locked
On the melting always-ahead
Arms parked by his side
His knees lift and drop
With a hip and a hop
'S-Joe' we kids call 'S-Joe'
Following him from one
End of town to the next
Keeping just out of reach
In case he springs
From his trance
Again I call 'S-Joe'
For his response
As I would have it
On his behalf 'S-Joe'
Shadowing him
My road tied to his name

59 (Spring 2008)

BILL MANHIRE

Velvet

The earliest deer had a number
and a name. And always when we called he came,
165, unlike those others in the paddock,
unlike the skyline or the failure
in the farmer's thumb, which slipped his mind
at some important moment. It is surely
the plural thing, pure need for company,
that makes us chant at the start of every story –
and in many poems, we say, the short line hides
within the longer. Now when they say velvet,
they mean blades and cuts, they mean this powder.
These days I spend my whole day planting trees.
For only a deer in solitude can be a 165,
can turn and be this other thing entire,
a great head watching from the wall.

59 (Spring 2008)

TOON TELLEGEN

A Man and an Angel:
studies for a poem

A man said:
I can't live,
and he lived long and meticulously

then he stood still and said:
I can't love,
and he loved women and peace
                    and unspoken shyness

and an angel descended, fought with him –
I can't fight, said the man
and he fought like a tiger, like a hare
                    and like a bag of bones

the sun went down and still they fought on,
the man and the angel,
and the man said:
now I know, I can't lose.

        *

Believe me, said an angel, I will save you,
no, said a man, I don't believe you,
you have to believe me, said the angel

and he drove away the ambition of the man
and his painful omniscience,
gave him peace
and large quantities of a rare, resilient happiness,
such as had never been described

do you believe me now, the angel asked
and he looked at the man with unparalleled love
and tenderness
and the man whispered: I don't believe you

        *

A man searched for his conscience
and an angel saw him and asked:
might this be it?
showed him a large and orthodox conscience

that is yours, said the man,
my conscience is grubby and full of holes –
but the angel shook his head:
we don't have a conscience,
we are too light,
we would fall,
we would lose from everyone,
we have only ourselves to contend with

and with a gesture of awesome insignificance
he struck the man down and dragged him away

and the man felt ashamed.

        *

In the end,
if we just wait long enough,
if we have seen beauty change shape,
if we have seen justice bend over backwards,
if we realise that we have believed in something
                    impossible,
if we have cherished hope to the point of madness,
if we have loved until we grew withered and
                    worm-eaten
and could not go on –
so help us what is left of our self-knowledge –
in the end,
out of everything that was
and could have been and should have been
in every fraction of our seconds,
there only remains
an I fighting with an angel,
night falls
and the angel strikes him down.

Translated from the Dutch by Judith Wilkinson

60 (Summer 2008)

MICHAEL SYMMONS ROBERTS

Man in a Fox Suit

Thin red hide, flea-ridden, caked
in mud and cack, thorn-snagged

he limps at dawn through bare-backed
woods, neck ricked and panic rising.

Tongue is purple, marked with plum
and elder, no, his mouth is brackish,

stained with bird blood. At odds
with the wild, this double-double spy

has tried to feign a genome mapped
to brushwood, amber, carrion.

He lives in terror of the true dogs
tearing him to pieces in defence

of mate or prey, to win his ground.
Vixen screams (in season now) beleaguer

his weak heart and I, sole witness, see
him rear up as a man, unlock a house

where he will stretch out in a warm
white bed and cast his rust coat

like an old rug on the floor.
He cannot help but hear the dog fox

after him with dry staccato barks,
rattling through skeletons of trees.

Fox in a Man Suit

Masked, gloved, brush tucked flat
against her back, faint with heat

this vixen is silent at soirées,
attentive to talk of defence, the public purse.

Emissary from the wild woods, agent
from the other side, she shakes her head

at wine, at canapés, she gags on human
stench, their meat and sweat.

When taxis come, she slips through kitchens,
drops to all fours (still in black tie),

sprints along the back streets
like a feral duke until she meets the edgelands

where – rubbed on the shuck of a tree –
her man-skin peels off

like a calyx and the sleek red flower unfurls.
Tongue drinks in the cold,

nose down in leaf mould, deep rush and tow
of attachment, of instinct. I, the only witness,

take this for a resurrection (body sloughed
and after-life as fox-soul), so I watch

in awe and slow my breath until
she catches sight and howls and howls.

60 (Summer 2008)

HELEN MORT

Rope

In the dream, there's still
a rope between us.

I know it by its warp;
the careful rope you used
to bind me at the breaking points
of my body – wrists
and ankles, fastened tight,
as if to keep me to myself;

rope you fixed
to anchor us to cliffs
in case your footholds gave
or I reached to pull against
a sloping door of rock
and opened it. Rope

that knew so much
of waiting; the floorboards
cold against my spine,
or outside, listening for the call
to climb – the slack brought in
the route set out before me.

Tonight, I'm bound to you again.
We've got so high, the city's turned
to patchwork. The rope's around
my waist, the other end
around your neck so tight
you'd barely know where flesh

begins. I grip the frame,
my knuckles white. I hold my breath
on every spur of rock.
You are running for the drop,
you're gathering speed,
you're sprinting for the break.

It will be years before
I feel the catch, and wake.

61 (Autumn 2008)

MARIANNE BORUCH

It isn't that serious before dawn, trees

It isn't that serious before dawn, trees
not pressed into service
by light yet. Birds are vague.
It's not the way

the violinist's A-string
breaks, middle of the cadenza.
Like my brother showed me
a view from the roof –

we didn't jump – then how
our childhood fit the nail he
pounded, for practice. Memory,
he said, take that. That's

a beginning. The first sound in woods
is alarm: *who walks here*. Soon all
quiets and continues. And I'll
be some other thing.

60 (Summer 2008)

EMMA JONES

Pietà

Baby, you sure look sick.
When I first held you that's what I thought,
this one won't last.

Everyone wanted a piece of you.
But I held you close, and the sky leaned in
all filled with rain, and those first-time

singers cleared their throats,
their hair all in the tops of trees and the motel signs.
See, I said, I've seen a sign!

and we pulled up on the escarpment
and ate fried food, and you took your breaths
in droplets, and drank so deep the streetlights spun
    with milk.

By morning you were thirty.
So gassed and shaken. A wind had caught itself
in you and couldn't get out.

Hey, I said, don't snag on his insides,
they're all he's got. But your heart shook like a guitar
that gets played and played

and only knows those songs,
the sorrow songs,
and you said 'sing to me'

and baby, I like to sing, so off we went,
and sang 'Love in the Museum'.
That's a good one, though it makes me cry.

See, I said, there's love in the museum!
I straightened out your fingers one by one.
You died, and your face stayed on the sheets.

I was restless then. I hate those nights.
You're heavy, baby.
The weight of a man in your bones.

Why you want the face of a man
with the face of a child?
Why have one and still the other?

You're small for a man. That's what they say.
They look at me funny.
Every eye naked as a highway

of bathers stretched by the pools on the motel roofs,
every one the same, one after the other,
while we looked for a place to lay our heads.

You sleepy now. I have a thing in me.
A bird or something.
It's cold, and knows the words of songs.

We sing now. Baby? You there?
I'm tired. I've seen your breath, flagged man.
You going now. Should we go. Baby?

61 (Autumn 2008)

JACK UNDERWOOD

Wilderbeast

In the wilderness the devil came to me:
big antique horns, a swinging red dick
and my father's angry voice.

He offered me grapes, a puckered teat
loose with wine and milk. I spat.
And he spat back, my mother's maiden name.

I pressed on, urged my feet. Satan changed tack;
swam me in sensation: my first time drunk,
the heat of a well spun lie, boyhood

glimpsed between a hairdresser's breasts,
the smell of shampoo and cigarette breath.
Then from a tuck in his arse he pulled rain

and a chip shop queue, the taste of shandy,
wet football boots dangled by the laces,
acorns and conkers tumbling from their spouts.

I gave a shout, a kind of grief escaping
and from astride his chin appeared
two slim girl's legs, akimbo his beard.

He opened his ripe mouth, folded his tongue back
and in, wriggling pleasure from himself,
stamping it out on the bare earth, braying.

I felt hunger folding in my gut.
The devil swung his hips, each jerk giving birth
to a pair of round, pert tits. *I am a good man!*

I railed and each flesh sack withered and slapped
on the ground, sizzled on the grit-heat of rock.
I heard waves, an ocean then. But it was Satan

shushing with a four-knuckled finger to his lips.
A breeze faltered and caught over, sea birds swung
in long arcs. The devil leaned in and touched me,

quietly, here and then here.
Softly he drew a perfect circle on the ground
bid me dream my mortal desire inside it.

I took out a photograph of you my love.
Showed him grace: fixed and flattened,
wrapped in a scarf and coat last week,

when the camera pinned you to the sea
and I watched it happen from behind the lens;
my breath holding you there a moment.

I showed the devil your photo and he wept.
Flies fell buzzing from his cheeks.
You tempted and turned him

and the sun strained to look
as the perfect circle became a pool of water,
hardened into a mirror,

the mirror I've been staring into since,
in our bathroom, in our flat,
with the wilderness of seconds between us.

61 (Autumn 2008)

DORA MALECH

Fair Play

Black rocks, red rocks.

White lichen and rot.

The trees wear
sleeves of moss.

The moss wears
a sheath of droplets
and a coat of fog.

The fog swans about
the valley until noon.

Then, wind, all
swither and swerve.

Some trick to sing
the breath away,
then swing back
in and sling it
through magnified
times more and more
so, oh troubled
ooh to the nth.

Sheet web
and spider
waits under.

Orb web
and spider waits
offstage with a leg
on a thread spun
from the center.

Grey warbler
hovers mid-air,
builds to a trill
that falls and rises,
plucks the spider
and the web as well,
harvests the thread
to bind less a nest
than a structure.

Rootlets, leaves, grass
coaxed and hung
bulb-shaped,
feather-lined.

Inside, two eggs.

The smaller is its own.

The larger, the cuckoo's
switcheroo, soon-to-be
insatiable foundling.

Mistletoe, too,
knows from opportune,
plants its seeds
to the bark
with a sticky kiss,
then settles in to suck
its host's sweet
everything.

Cat takes to
the woods, can't see
her penance, but
smells it close.

Her owner has tied
the dead finch
tight to her collar,
broken neck to neck.

The faster she runs,
the more it flaps
against her throat.

Fiddleheads unfurl
fractal, furred fronds
curl their hearts out,
a million question
marks set to the sun
and soon to exclaim
all the way open.

Fleet of spiderlings
unspools to catch
and be caught by
the current, wind
which lifts the strings
and scatters, drops
the bodies a-field
like leaflets too tiny
for proper propaganda,
more like prayers
inscribed on
grains of rice –

let us at least attempt
our impossibly
tiny lives.

64 (Autumn 2009)

BRIGIT PEGEEN KELLY

The Philosophers

Today the Bay is blue, blue, blue –
it looks like a mountain lake, icy water
that goes down and down and does not stop –

it does not look like a basin of water
so shallow it can be waded across, or if
the tide is out, walked across – though

it is a very long walk, for the Bay
is big and wide – ten miles from East to West,
ten miles from South to North – and a walk

only the birds will hazard because
the pink mud is so soft and deep
one step forward will bring you to your knees.

But the birds can walk on the mud, the birds do –
lifting their delicate feet, turning their
delicate heads – and just before the tide

is fully out, or just after it has begun
to swing back in, when a thin sheet of water
slides green and soundless across

the mud, the long-legged birds
seem to be walking not on mud but on water,
like little Jesuses – the wide Bay

becomes a city of little Jesuses, stepping
this way and that, thinking their
deep thoughts, or bending down

to write on the water, or standing
for imponderable spells perfectly still –
as if they have lost their way.

63 (Summer 2009)

PAUL FARLEY

Google Earth

Now I'm a hand setting the globe to spin,
finding a country, starting to zoom in
now I'm an eye. Now I'm a meteorite.

The scars of business corridors, the white
clay works, national parkland, estuaries.
A refinery built from Camemberts and Bries!

Now I'm a hand again, steadying my fall,
steering by starlight on the ground, black holes
of reservoirs, flight paths of major roads.

Now I'm an eye and there are never clouds
because the west wind of the Internet
blows silently down lost bus routes, birth streets,

the school roof still in bad need of repair,
the swing park all deserted at this hour,
which is no-hour. Now I'm the midnight sun

lighting the places where we've been and gone.
The ground comes up. A field sharpens to grain.
The trees screw into leaf. Now I'm a drop of rain.

Now I'm a balloon by Odilon Redon.
And now my chute snags up on power-lines.
If we looked outside, eyeballs might block the sun.

Even above the lake isles of Lough Gill,
Adlestrop's dismantled barrow, a hill
on the road north of Poughkeepsie, there are eyes

now all the world's a drop zone of the mind.

63 (Summer 2009)

PAUL BATCHELOR

To a Halver

And the little screaming fact that sounds through all history...
— John Steinbeck

O halver, O haffa, O half-brick: your battened-down
century of faithful service in a pit village terrace
forgotten now you've broken loose; now you're at large
on CCTV, flackering out of kilter till you bounce
like far-flung hail rebounding off the riot squad –
or kissing the away support a fond goodbye –
or anyhow let fly, as fifty years ago
someone aimed you at my father's skull
while he was being shepherded down Rutherglen Road
when it was raining bottles, when it was raining hammers and nails
after an Old Firm fixture – the decider: I exist
because you missed and broke his collarbone –
I weigh you now against the good you've done.
St George's Hill, when Cromwell's cavalry advance
we find you, or your country cousins, apt and good,
versatile in the hands of the True Levellers;
now Banksy has a laugh replacing you with flowers;
and what about your bit-part in that dockyard stand-off?
The gates swing-to, the scabs clock on –
as to the nitty-gritty of whose side you're on,
you stay, as they say, ahead of the curve.
But you were there at Peterloo and you were there
at Brixton. You were all the rage in Meadowell.
Your ancestors were with us in the cave
before the wheel before the fire and ever since
we've never been without you: all our grand designs
can be reduced to you. You stand for stunted hope
grown wild among the backyard odds and sods
where the snubbed toaster and the jilted BMX
jockey for position with the unacknowledged honesty.
O root and seed of boxed-in lives! O token of dissent!
How often have I seen you in the thick of it
and raised my arm against you? On pitted tarmac,
by the gutted community centres of besieged estates –
borne as a gift or hurled down like a prophecy –
I've seen you taken up and even in the playground,
hidden in a snowball, you followed hard upon.
You've come a long way from the clay-pit, worked out and abandoned;
a long way from the vanished kilns of Langley and Eldon –

here: let me launch you on another posthumous career,
earthbound comet, stub of destiny, throwback. I have a
soft spot for you, so go on: make something happen,
O clod, O totem of the unaccommodated, O halver –
history's ellipsis point, sign to which we must attend –
when words fail may you always be at hand.

64 (Autumn 2009)

CAROL ANN DUFFY

Scheherazade

Dumb was as good as dead;
better to utter.
Inside a bottle, a genie.
Abracadabra.
Words were a silver thread
stitching the night.
The first story I said
led to the light.

Fact was in black and white;
fiction was colour.
Inside a dragon, a jewel.
Abracadabra.
A magic carpet took flight,
bearing a girl.
The hand of a Queen shut tight
over a pearl.

Imagination was world;
clever to chatter.
Inside a she-mule, a princess.
Abracadabra.
A golden sword was hurled
into a cloud.
A dead woman unfurled
out of a shroud.

A fable spoken aloud
kindled another.
Inside a virgin, a lover.
Abracadabra.
Forty thieves in a crowd,
bearded and bold.
A lamp rubbed by a lad
turning to gold.

Talking lips don't grow cold;
babble and jabber.
Inside a turkey, a fortune.
Abracadabra.
What was lost was held
inside a tale.
The tall stories I told
utterly real.

Inside a marriage, a gaol;
better to vanish.
Inside a mirror, an ogre;
better to banish.
A thousand and one tales;
weeping and laughter.
Only the silent fail.
Abracadabra.

64 (Autumn 2009)

C.K. WILLIAMS

Jew On Bridge

Raskolnikov hasn't slept. For days. In his brain, something like white.
A wave stopped in mid-leap. Thick, slow, white. Or maybe it's brain.
Brain in his brain. Old woman's brain on the filthy floor of his brain.

His destiny's closing in. He's on his way, we're given to think, though
he'll have to go first through much suffering, to punishment, then redemption.
Love, too. Punishment, love, redemption; it's all mixed up in his brain.

Can't I go back to my garret, to my filthy oil-cloth couch, and just sleep?
That squalid neighborhood where he lived. I was there. Whores, beggars,
derelict men with flattened noses: the police break their noses on purpose.

Poor crumpled things. He can't, though, go back to his filthy garret.
Rather this fitful perambulation. Now we come to a bridge on the Neva.
Could you see the sea from there then? I think I saw it from there.

Then, on the bridge, hanging out of the plot like an arm from a car,
no more function than that in the plot, car, window, arm, even less,
there, on the bridge, purposeless, plotless, not even a couch of his own: Jew.

On page something or other, chapter something, Raskolnikov sees JEW.
And takes a moment, a break, you might say, from his plot, from his fate,
his doom, to hate him, the Jew, loathe, despise, want him not *there*.

Jew. Not as in Chekhov's ensemble of Jews wailing for a wedding.
Not Chekhov, dear Chekhov. Dostoevsky instead, whom I esteemed
beyond almost all who ever scraped with a pen, but who won't give the Jew,

miserable Jew, the right to be short, tall, thin or fat Jew: just Jew.
Something to distract you from your shuttering tunnel of fate, your memory,
consciousness, loathing, self-loathing, knowing the slug you are.

What's the Jew doing anyway on that bridge on the beautiful Neva?
Maybe he's Paul, as in Celan. Antschel-Celan, who went over the rail of a bridge.
Oh my *Todesfuge*, Celan is thinking. The river's not the Neva, but the Seine.

It's the bridge on the Seine where Jew-poet Celan is preparing himself.
My *Deathfugue*. My black milk of daybreak. Death-master from Germany.
Dein goldenes Haar Marguerite. Dein aschenes Haar Sulamith. Aschenes-Antschel.

Was it sunrise, too, as when Raskolnikov, sleepless, was crossing his bridge?
Perhaps sleepless is why Raskolnikov hates this Jew, this Celan, this Antschel.
If not, maybe he'd love him. Won't he love the prisoners in his camp?

Won't he love and forgive and cherish the poor girl he's been tormenting?
Christian forgiveness all over the place, like brain on your boot.
Though you mustn't forgive, in your plot, Jew on bridge; Deathfugue on bridge.

Celan-Antschel goes over the rail. As have many others before him.
There used to be nets down near Boulogne to snare the debris, the bodies,
of prostitutes, bankrupts, sterile young wives, gamblers, and naturally Jews.

Celan was so sick of the *Deathfugue* he'd no longer let it be printed.
In the tape of him reading, his voice is songful and fervent, like a cantor's.
When he presented the poem to some artists, they hated the way he recited.

His parents had died in the camps. Of typhus the father. Mama probably gun.
Celan-Antschel had escaped. He'd tried to convince them to come, too.
Was that part of it, on the bridge? Was that he wrote in German part, too?

He stood on the bridge over the Seine, looked into the black milk of dying,
Jew on bridge, and hauled himself over the rail. *Dein aschenes Haar...*
Dostoevsky's Jew, though, is still there. On page something or other.

He must be waiting to see where destiny's plotting will take him. It won't.
He'll just have to wait there forever. Jew on bridge, hanging out of the plot.
I try to imagine what he would look like. My father? Grandfathers? Greats?

Does he wear black? Would he be like one of those hairy Hasids
where Catherine buys metal for her jewelry, in their black suits and hats,
even in summer, *shvitzing*, in the heat? Crackpots, I think. They depress me.

Do I need forgiveness for my depression? My being depressed like a Jew?
All right then: how Jewish am I? What portion of who I am is a Jew?
I don't want vague definitions, qualifications, here on the bridge of the Jew.

I want certainty, *science*: everything you are, do, think; think, do, are,
is precisely twenty-two percent Jewish. Or six and a half. Some nice prime.
Your suffering is Jewish. Your resistant, resilient pleasure in living, too,

can be tracked to some Jew on some bridge on page something or other
in some city, some village, some shtetl, some festering *shvitz* of a slum,
with Jews with black hats or not, on their undershirts fringes or not.

Raskolnikov, slouching, shoulders hunched, hands in his pockets,
stinking from all those sleepless nights on his couch, clothes almost rotting,
slouching and stinking and shivering and muttering to himself, plods on

past the Jew on the bridge, who's dressed perhaps like anyone else –
coat, hat, scarf, boots – whatever. Our hero would recognize him
by his repulsive, repellent Jew-face daring to hang out in the air.

My father's name also was Paul. As in Celan. His father's name: Benjamin.
As in Walter. Who flung himself from life, too, with vials of morphine.
In some hotel from which he could have reached safety but declined to.

Chose not to. Make it across. Though in fact none of us makes it across.
Aren't we all in that same shitty hotel on that bridge in the shittiest world?
What was he thinking, namesake of my grandpa? Benjamin, Walter, knew all.

Past, future, all. He could see perfectly clearly the death he'd miss out on.
You're in a room. Dark. You're naked. Crushed on all sides by others naked.
Flesh-knobs. Hairy or smooth. Sweating against you. *Shvitzing* against you.

Benjamin would have played it all out in his mind like a fugue. Deathfugue.
The sweating, the stinking. And that moment you know you're going to die,
and the moment past that, which, if you're Benjamin, Walter, not grandpa,

you know already by heart: the searing through you you realize is your grief,
for humans, all humans, their world and their cosmos and oil-cloth stars.
All of it worse than your fear and grief for your own minor death.

So, gulp down the morphine quickly, because of your shame for the humans,
what humans can do to each other. Benjamin, grandfather, Walter;
Paul, father, Celan: all the names that ever existed wiped out in shame.

Celan on his bridge. Raskolnikov muttering Dostoevsky under his breath.
Jew on bridge. Raskolnikov-Dostoevsky still in my breath. Under my breath.
Black milk of daybreak. *Aschenes Haar*. Antschel-Celan. Ash. Breath.

65 (Spring 2010)

JO SHAPCOTT

Somewhat Unravelled

Auntie stands by the kettle, looking at the kettle
and says, help me, help me, where is the kettle?
I say, little auntie, the curlicues and hopscotch grids
unfurling in your brain have hidden it from you. Let me
make you a cup of tea. She says ah ha! But I do
my crossword, don't I, OK not the difficult one, the one
with the wasname? Cryptic clues. Not that. I say,
auntie, little auntie, we were never cryptic
so let's not start now. I appreciate your straight-on talk,
the built-up toilet seats, the way you wish poetry
were just my hobby, our cruises on the stair lift,
your concern about my weight, the special seat in the bath.
We know where we are. She says, nurse told me
I should furniture-walk around the house, holding on to it.
I say, little auntie you are a plump armchair
in flight, a kitchen table on a difficult hike without boots,
you do the sideboard crawl like no one else, you are a sofa
rumba, you go to sleep like a rug. She says,
I don't like eating. Just as well *you've* got
a good appetite. I say littlest auntie, my very little auntie
(because she is shrinking now, in front of me)
let me cook for you, a meal so wholesome and blimmin'
pungent with garlic you will dance on it and
eat it through your feet. Then she says don't you
ever want to go to market and get lost
in pots, fruit and random fabric? Don't you
want to experiment with rain, hide out in storms,
cover your body with a layer only one raindrop
thick? Don't you want to sell your nail-clippings
online? She says, look at you, with all your language,
you never became the flower your mother
wanted but it's not too late, come with me
and rootle in the earth outside my front window,
set yourself in the special bed, the one only
wasname is allowed to garden and we will practise
opening and closing and we'll follow the sun
with our faces until the cows come home.

65 (Spring 2010)

SHARON OLDS

Sleekit Cowrin'

When a caught mouse lay dead, for a week,
and stuck to the floor, I started setting
the traps on a few of my ex's and my old
floral salad plates. Late
one night, when I see one has sprung, I put it on the
porch, to take it to the woods in the morning, but by
morning I forget, and by noon – and by after-
noon the Blue Willow's like a charnel roof
in Persia when the bodies of the dead were put for the
scholar vultures to pick the text
of matter and the text of spirit apart.
The mouse has become a furry barrow
burrowed into by a beetle striped
in stripes of hot and stripes of cold
coal – head-first, it eats its way in
to the heart sweeter than dirt, to the mouse-bowels
saltier, beeswax and soap
stopped in the small intestinal channels.
And bugs little as seeds are seething
all over the hair, as if the rodent
were food rejoicing. And the Nicrophorous
cuts and thrusts, it rocks and rolls
its tomentose muzzle, and its wide shoulders,
in. And I know, I know, I should put
my dead marriage out on the porch
in the sun, and let who can, come
and nourish of it – change it, carry it
back to what it was assembled from,
back to the source of the light whereby it shone.

66 (Summer 2010)

JULIAN STANNARD

Don't Die

My soul is humming along the Thames
is an ill-advised way to begin a poem
unless you're Keats or overcome by
such a Keatsian swoon
which on a day like this near Pimlico
when you're strolling by the river
offering your heart to Lambeth Palace
is not so difficult to believe.

I saw a lot of blood in the hospital.
I used to staunch the blood
and truth to say I was a specialist
when it came to blood. In fact it is
the word which rhymes most perfectly
with flood and on a day like this
near Vauxhall I am waiting for the river's
gaudy ink to splash against the banks.

See me clutching arteries!
St Thom's, hospital of blood
I cannot recognize it but that was where
the painful contract was beaten out
which served me well and served me ill:
pulse, poetry, pulmonary visions.

My soul is humming along the Thames
and I am drifting in and out of Fanny
is an ill-advised way of continuing a poem
unless you're dying or dead or feel
a magpie standing on your heart which
on a day like this on the banks of the river
when all that's left is a summer breeze
is not so difficult to believe.

From under the surface of the Thames
the dead are blowing bubbles:
imagine phalanges of men and women and
little children all dressed in sartorial black
and so perfectly choreographed.
They want to sing but when they open
their lungs they send a great volley
of bubbles to the world which cannot see them.

66 (Summer 2010)

ANGIE ESTES

Shade

As the air full of rain takes on rainbow
hues not of its own making but reflecting
the brightness of another, so the soul
of a shade, Statius explains to Dante
in Purgatory, is made visible like flame
following the shift and flicker of
its fire: the soul imprints itself
on the surrounding air to make it
resemble, reassemble the memory
of its body, just as the six hundred foot high
sandstone walls marbled in shades of
pink, of rose and red, and sometimes
veined in cobalt blue remember
the chasm of the Siq, the city of Petra
carved in its side. Copper – from Latin *cuprum*,
'from Cyprus' – in ancient times was mined
on the island of Cyprus, and the Greek
kutuhlpa meant 'head with wings,' so the unclaimed
cremated remains of those known as
the incurably insane at Oregon State Hospital
were sealed in copper canisters and placed
in an underground vault, forgotten and flooded
for fifteen years. Mold or lichen, phosphorescent
frost? A host of ashes coats the copper: cuprite,
azurite, malachite turn to verdigris, turquoise, atoll
green and the lapis lazuli seas of Hokusai seen
from outer space, the white seam of a shoreline
at every tropical copper beach, where the long news
of the body finally breaks. Like a necklace
at the edge of saline or alkaline lakes, crust
of flour on the fingers or powder after surgical gloves
peel off, the pollen of catalpa blossoms remained
on the tips long after our fingers slid
past the purple spots and yellow flares
into each white frilly, unfurled urn:
we plucked them from the green-hearted
leaves, chanting *witches' fingers, heads
with wings*, our hands held up like the claws
of Hokusai's *Great Wave*, like St. Francis
receiving the stigmata or the hands
my grandmother raised when she looked up
after she had finished kneading dough.

66 (Summer 2010)

Brief Encounter

The story is *the only one*
                        I can tell and the only one I can

                        never tell, she says after she has left
her lover for the last time, in voiceover

to her husband, *the only one I can tell*
                        and the only one I can never

                        tell. 'So help me with this,'
he says, 'you're a poetry addict –

it's Keats: "When I behold
                        upon the night's starred face

                        huge cloudy symbols of
a high _____" ... seven letters,

beginning with *r.*' *reading regalia*
                        rosette rotunda royalty rapture I didn't think

                        such violent things could happen
to ordinary people, she says, *radiant*

raccoon, ravelled rivulet raiment
                        release although weeks ago she and her lover

                        sat in a dark theatre and watched the preview
of a film announced in flickering font

on the screen: *Flames of Passion – Coming*
                        Shortly. The chords of Rachmaninoff draw dark

                        lines across their faces, cancel
conversation like the diagonal trains

that slice the rectangular frames of film
                        in two as they arrive and depart

                        from Milford Junction station which, once
the lovers kiss, becomes a soundproof

room *reprise redwing refusal, recount rhubarb*
                        reserve, reverse rustles refrain Hurrying

home in the train she sees her face
facing her face in the window, racing

with darkened trees like the fragrant
pages of a rampant book.

66 (Summer 2010)

KATHRYN MARIS

Street Sweeper

God scatters where he eats.
The sweeper wheels his cart to what falls.

The broom assembles a pile.
The wind dismantles the pile.

God is the messy wind. The pile
is the mouthpiece of the wind.

Sometimes the wind is bluster.
Sometimes the wind is a mute.

There is the God who listens.
There is the God who speaks.

The God who listens is a gentle liar.
The God who speaks is laconic and hard.

I ask if I'm loved.
He points to the graveyard his garden abuts.

I clutch his hair. I say *Am I loved?*
He claims his love for me is deep

but zealless. Over the garden wall,
the God who listens, the neighbour,

smiles when I ask if I am loved.
He points to the God across the wall,

the first God, the God I just left,
as if to say *God loves you*.

Sometimes he speaks through his dog.
Sometimes he doesn't speak.

If his mother tongue were 'dog'
or 'frog' or 'wind' or 'rubbish'

could I learn that language
and hear that I was loved?

Or would the answer
be something I couldn't hear.

The Periodic Table won't revoke
what it has put in the world:

earth metals, non-metals, catalysts.
It is God's slovenly generosity

and is difficult to gather,
as the street sweeper knows,

as the wind knows, as I know, and God knows.
The sweeper smiles at me lovingly

like the silent god,
the one with the message I cannot hear.

66 (Summer 2010)

TOBY MARTINEZ DE LAS RIVAS

Covenant

Say the truth. Northumberland as Israel. Parts of it prefigured as the Shulamite woman.

Hebron, hard by Haltwhistle.

Blessèd Robert Westall, at the texts of *The Plague House* and *Machine Gunners*.
The grey hull of Resurre.

Or *The Wind Eye*, in these fallen days.

Reading this text to my sons, as if wading through harl into hís strange, apostolic light.

O, Shulamite.

It ís a wild fucking kingdom.

Surface bewildered by the risen heads of seals, a sea trout's dorsal arc. The thistle,
garishly arrayed, rehearses its gospel crowned in flame.

World, split between shod and unshod.

The King of Scotland, dead.

Terror and counter-terror, broken walls littering the dominion,
the high woe of bairns like seal-pups.

Marram grass soup,
no less.

I must bend my knee to hím again.

Clouds shift like tercels ínland, úpland, wést to Gateshead, and the rain in its vehemence

67 (Autumn 2010)

MEDBH McGUCKIAN

The Meaning of Margaret's Hands

'You – are you – isn't it all the same?'
Her lived space is a match burning in a crocus.
Sunk flatly in on the landing, she slumps
Listless, saddened, patient as cattle,
And concentrates on holding her smile in place.

She might be looking down, not across,
The way a curtain hangs and stirs
Beyond a surging diagonal of long-necked flowers,
Their breasts sky-blue.
Her slightly poisonous, wasp-yellow cushion intrudes
So her slope-shouldered shadow has leaked out
In a strand of amber.

She seems eaten away by the air that surrounds her,
Draws her fluid shawl about her to one side
Like a sainted, earthen person.
A bracelet that tastes salty repeatedly falls down
On her wrist, where her finger and thumb
Serve as sugar-tongs with muted purple
Underlights in her fingernails.

She is twisted forward down into herself,
The weight of her torso supported like a wheelbarrow.
Her breasts, that let themselves be searched for,
Shift and swing in the enormous dress
With its puffs and bell-skirts.
She carries them like a purse
So the outline of her ribs screens any gaze
Upon them, she rests them through the peach
Of her heart on a dilapidated pillow.

When the day-bell sounds or the wine-bell
Shuts the taverns, her chair becomes a lap
For the tissue tension of her heavy thighs.
She lays her face on the water of a vase
Located around her head. A switch
Of acid colour within her cut-open eye
Grazes the alert forcelines of her hair.

As her hands are taken from her, handed over
Like the lightest foot of a footed bowl
To which we give the name 'Care' and unpack it.

Something as mobile as a human being
Gives that roundabout kiss to the keepsake
Of her lungs where every window
Shuddered the withoutness of the obliterated hotel
While children were being born.

67 (Autumn 2010)

NICHOLA DEANE

My Moriarty

Up on the Reichenbach Falls, Moriarty,
just you, me and a flattering rainbow-hued
nimbus of mist. You with that spidery voice,
all machinating, echoey, hoaxy-coaxy,
or the ursine growl you use to show who's boss.
I've been onto you for years, one step behind,
not quite solving you, my darling conundrum.
And still I wake at night wondering whether
I could pick you out in a line-up. Doubtful,
I know, when I've only ever glimpsed you, *profil
perdu*, slipping through the crowds of extras
in the overpopulated palaces of dream.
Yet I'd swear I've memorized the contour of your cheekbone,
mentally sketched the curve of your right eye-socket,
the way the corner of your mouth lifts when you smirk
having foiled me again. Bored of defeat,
my God, how I want you facing me at last,
your phiz inked in, not smudged in charcoal,
glimpsed in mirrors, or flickering from passing trains.
You who are coat-tails, teasing letters in code,
the man who paid up and left just moments ago,
let's agree for once you'll skip all that.
Of course, we'll need some rules to make it sporting,
like momentary presence, eye contact –
but nothing that smacks of the future, of staying forever.
So trust me. Relax. You'll like what I do when I catch you.
And of course you can slip the knots I'll tie but not
before, in the tussle of the denouement, you try
the ways I've found to make you shout my name.

69 (Summer 2011)

JAMIE McKENDRICK

King Billy's Nemesis

Mouldywarp, thrower of dirt,
has tripped the horse called Sorrel
and broken the royal collarbone and killed
the King of England.

Though Jacobites toasted the little gentleman
in the black velvet waistcoat,
if push came to shove he was always
more of a Republican

and apart from a walk-on role
as the ghost of King Hamlet
till then he'd rarely shown
much passion for politics.

Three hundred years he's laid low,
airing the earth and stocking his larder
with shelf-fulls of worms,
live worms as it happens.

But today he broached the deep snow
and left one flaw in the perfect
field of white – black earth
at its core and an oval

aureole of cindery grey
with an equal mix of snow and soil.
Looks like a black wig
riding a white steed.

Now he's backed up down into the dark,
same old mole, with a bow and a scrape
or was that a wave
from his shovel-shaped mitt?

69 (Summer 2011)

SAMANTHA WYNNE-RHYDDERCH

Vive la Résistance!

It was on such a night as this that I floated
like a débutante into the arms of a cornfield
outside Rouen, my parachute silks streaming
into a bridal train adorning the corn

and for the first time I felt the full weight
of what it must be to be a woman always
dragging a dress through obtuse fields. So I
unharnessed myself from the lot, rolled up

my folds and ran off to the lychgate
of Sainte Marie du Chêne where I awaited
an assignation with a Monsieur Lefas
who passed me a map in a cigarette packet

which I followed to a farm to be met by
a frowning chap in breeches who unhooked
the door of a barn where his daughter was
hitching up a bed for me in linsey-woolsey.

At the altar I hovered between doubt
and belief until she glided down the aisle
stitched into my parachute and for a second
we soared above the priest, the spire,

the higgledy fields, the two of us threaded
together in the silks that had saved me, which I later
unbuttoned and she has since trapped in the attic
in case one day they take off without us.

69 (Summer 2011)

SEAN O'BRIEN

The Lost Book

Here's where the far-gone Irish came to die
And having died got up to disappear
Into the space they wore into the air:
Smoke-room, bookie's, God knows where –
They were a crowd who favoured solitude.
They came 'pro tem' and stayed, and stayed,
Bed-sitting room remittance-men
Whose files authority had usefully mislaid.
Dug out of 'kiln-baked' tombs, the gas left on,
This Tendency the calendar forgot
Kept suitcases of ancient paperwork
That could have grassed them up but didn't talk.
Poor demi-felons, dead of what? – of afternoons,
Whose rag and bone the council boxed and burned:
And you were of their party, were you not?

I owe you this. I watched you and I learned.
You lived provisionally, 'the man with no home team'.
Reliant on the Masonry of drink, you made
A modest and convincing entryist of crowds
Who only ever knew your Christian name,
Your trebles at Uttoxeter, perhaps
Your politics, on no account your game.
You seemed composed entirely of words.
'Tell no man – still less a woman – who you are.'
Who cares, now that the principals are dead
As the impossible morality
Whose prohibitions brought your lie to life
And in the end would send you off your head?
I care, for I was made to care.
You told a priest but couldn't tell your wife.
You were the author and the patient too,
And in another life another house
Imprisoned others and the clock had stopped.

You knew – and all you did was know –
That there was an appointment to be kept.
That was your art – to frame your punishment –
An endlessly extended sentence,
Solitary confinement in plain sight,
Nothing you could put down on the page,
Nothing you could ever simply name
But manifest in jealousy and rage
And episodes of heartbroken repentance.
There was nothing that could ever put it right.

'Yourself's a secret thing – take care of it,
But if it comes to handy grips you take no shit.'
Yours was a way of waiting, though you knew
That really there was nothing down for you
But vestibules and corridors and days
In which to seek permission to be old.
Kardomah Lampedusa, minus book,
Deported from successive realms of gold –
Longpavement and the Bronx and Hammersmith –
Or so you said, and who was I to ask?
Then when at last I came to take a look,
When you had sat it out as far as death,
Inside the case, behind the broken lock,
There were no secrets waiting underneath,
Just fragments of a poem you'd recite,
And scraps of stories you'd begun and re-begun,
In which the names alone would change, as though
You had forgotten who they were.

I found no history in this, no hidden world
Before I came – I'd heard your stuff bashed out
Through years of chainsmoked afternoons
And read it when you asked me to. I liked
The one where in the fog the sergeant found
His constable nailed up across a five-bar gate,
But feared and did not understand the priest
In his deserted parish (fog again)
Who found his name had changed to Lucifer.
He lost his way and then he lost his mind
And that was that, with nowhere left to go,
Hell being where and who and what he was,
A state with neither origin nor end.

'The duty is to entertain,' you said, 'or else
To seek to make no sense at all'. And then
When you had filled the room with ash and smoke
There would be racing or the news, a second
Scouring of the *Telegraph*, a third, and no
Persuading you that you should persevere.
You were already old. Was that the plan?
To climb into the box and disappear
In smoke above the crematorium
And leave your furious pursuers unappeased
And shorn of purpose, standing in the snow
Beside the hearse, in mourning for themselves?

I studied you before the lid was sealed
And, as my mother had requested, placed
Rosemary for remembrance in your hands.
The deep, unhappy brow, the cloud-white hair
Combed back – oh, you were otherwise engaged.
In settling debts, or simply free to dream?
You wouldn't care to comment 'at this stage'.
Was there another world, where you belonged,
Or one more corridor where you still sit, rereading
With the patience of a lifetime
Last week's paper, hoping it might yield
To scrutiny and show the outcome changed?

67 (Autumn 2010)

Faun Whistling to a Blackbird

This afternoon a blackbird came to my nook
while I was sleeping off a feed of goat curds
and retsina. I'd rented one of those dreams
from Morpheus in which I was roughing it
with A down the Glens – or was it her cousin X?
The bird startled me as she foraged near my kit,
amongst the mosses where notepad and pen
had slipped from my hand. Maybe she mistook
the pad for bread since the pages were white
with some crumbs about growing old and sex?
She took flight, but only as far as the eglantine
behind my head. I tootled to her, *Sweet bird,*
why abuse a poet lost amid his fuzzy dreams…
She whistled back, some Goidelic curse she'd heard
beside the Erne or Belfast Lough. Such a flyting
we had, such a duel or duet we struck up then
as my brains fired, two heated creatures reared
in wind and muck becoming soul-companions
under the Sicilian sun – her feathered, me furred.

68 (Spring 2011)

JAN WAGNER

from eighteen pies

Thence to dinner to Sir W Pen's, it being a solemn feast day with him, his wedding day, and we had, besides a good chine of beef and other good cheer, eighteen mince pies in a dish, the number of the years that he hath been married.
— The Diary of Samuel Pepys

Anything you can think of can be made into a pie, and a capable chef can irrefutably demonstrate his imagination and good judgement through the combinations he chooses.
— Carl Friedrich von Rumohr,
The Spirit of the Culinary Arts

1. (shepherd's pie)

sheep are clouds that love the ground.
the shepherd loves marie. he scatters nuts
on the hillside, whispering the three famous words.
the herd bleats, devours them like white writing
on a green chalkboard. behind them bounds the period,
the sheepdog. in the valley they draw
evening shadows across the windows. they
see neither the hillside, nor the hills, nor the clouds.
clouds are sheep driven away by the wind.

4. (cheese and onion pastries)

*I have a heart of stone, say men,
but what do they know of stones.*
— Maria Barnas

what i know of stones is their weight
in the belly of a wolf or of a well,
echoing after the drop; one night in may,
i thought i saw them on a cliff,
sunk in thought, moonlit and pale
like onions. but what do i know of onions,
of their gown of skins and the heart,
that burning, which peels away layer by layer.

5. (genueser gemüsepastetchen)

I

winding through the hours before the ferry
left, through side alleys
near the harbour. you vanished into a shoe
shop. under the hooves of the noon
heat, wrecked by that dream
of too much water, i saw the shadows,
the saints in their interval of stone, ossified
in their good deeds. nothing decided.
the hawker's dried fish all strung up salty, stiff,
like fetishes, the blue fish high up on the line.
the dragon might as well have scoffed
at george, leaning on his lance,
a tired worker with his spade.

II

corsica
is said to be recognisable by its scent, long
before the island itself surfaces from the sea.

7. (terrine de poulet au foie de volaille)

cackling, the hen scurries after the mystery
of self, you said, just like us.
whatever that means. the hen is
white. it stares at the cropped sky, the dust
in which it is allowed to fly, the ground
on which a firmament of grain has been sprinkled
for it. it knows only this: before day's end
it will bury its red comb under speckled
wings, and sleep until dawn.
the night is in it, as its greed for corn
and millet shows. in its stomach, the seed traces
its cycles in deep darkness
and disappears into space, only to return
again. on a single grain sits a tiny hut
with a bed in it. look – from under the eiderdown,
your naked foot peeks out.

9. (empanada)

it was not africa, it was a rock
in water at best, she said. white
villages in the rearview mirror, inert
like glaciers – the sky was light,
as though it carried its own weight.
in the rearview mirror, the sierra
with its peaks, beneath it a sura
of cork oaks. how the wind tossed
her hair. before us lay the sea, which
said yes, then no, to the beach.
it was not a rock, it was a continent.

16. (apple pie)

Ah, happy, happy boughs!
– John Keats

an april morning, still studded with stars when she
stepped to the window – roused from last
night's dreams by the sibilance of the anti-frost
sprinkler – below her yesterday's valley, an empty

ballroom glistening beneath a dome of dusk,
the apple trees green and encrusted
with ice, suspended like crystal
chandeliers. in the corral

next door, two foals stand motionless in the glow
of this cold splendour. further away in the half
light, the lamppost at a bus stop,
the sign, its intense, florid yellow.

Translated from the German by Chenxin Jiang

68 (Spring 2011)

KATHLEEN JAMIE

Hawk and Shadow

I watched a hawk
glide low across the hill,
her own dark shape
in her talons like a kill.

She tilted her wings,
fell into the air –
the shadow coursed on
without her, like a hare.

Being out of sorts
with my so-called soul,
part unhooked hawk,
part shadow on parole

I played fast and loose:
keeping one in sight
while forsaking the other.
The hawk gained height:

her mate on the ground
began to fade,
till hill and sky were empty,
and I was afraid.

70 (Autumn 2011)

AHREN WARNER

from Metousiosis

Look, sometimes it happens my hands become aware
of each other, or my worn out face seeks shelter
in them. Then I feel a slight sensation.
But who'd dare to exist just for that?
                                    – Rainer Maria Rilke,
                        The Duino Elegies: Second Elegy

L'avocat, 1866

As, between Delphi and Thebes, where *rāmus*
turns to *rāmulī*, old Oedipus shafts Laius

good and proper, batters him with his staff
then finishes the King (and his coterie) off...

And as, leaving the codger dead at the road's crotch,
he never looks back or gives it a second thought

but, instead, makes his way to Thebes, to years
of plenty, to night after night of shafting his mother

(that is, until she tops herself, until he digs
his own eyes out)...

          So, you happen upon your leg
or arm, and your flesh is *unhomely*: a waxed rind,

a terrine of silt and scud.

Sitzender Männlicher Akt, 1910

'... the stain of blood makes shipwreck of our state'
slips drowsily into 'shipwrecked in this sea is sweet

to me'. The night presses through the shutters' slats.
Parasomnic, one finger skims the sternum's flat

then draws an ellipse from plexus to armpit
and back; arcs off and up to circle my upper lip.

So many nights I wake to find myself like this,
tracing the contours of my self – near catatonic –

one hand puppeteered and seeking the spots
where nerves hustle or a coarse down bristles;

where, beneath the glaze of *cogitans*, touch
can trigger surety – flesh and bone assurance –

          beyond this party trick of intellect.

Le Boeuf Écorché, 1924

And sure, who could miss the significance
of Rembrandt's *Le Boeuf Écorché*, his cow carcass

strung up, crucified, painted on its stand?
The word became flesh, made his dwelling among us

etcetera. Except, as Soutine knows so well,
there is no *logos* here; the muscle and sinew

sag silently. There is only flesh and shadow,
a hush of bone, wilting skin and gristle.

The same silence throbs in Soutine's rendition
con fuoco (as Rembrandt's nose also throbs

in that self-portrait, puce and drink-pocked).
The carrion insists, exists as an affirmation,

as a reverie of flesh become flesh become fleshy.

1947-J, 1947

after Baudelaire

Darling, do you remember that sweet morning
down a shortcut for fear of fair-weather tourists

we came upon a carcass rotting, its legs spread
like an easy girl, nonplussed, gut swollen, stinking?

The sun beat down, blazed radiant, as if to roast,
to serve it up in its own pustulant dripping.

The bleary sky watched the carrion blossoming,
maggots pooling among tattered jerky, dry crud.

A bitch eyed us, skulked and slathered. Not if
but when, my solace, you too end up like this,

then tell the grubs and parasites that kiss
and nibble at your face, I've vouched safe

       the form and essence of our love.

Head of J.Y.M II, 1984–85

The same raised head, same elegant carotid
– bared and throbbing – unite both Jocasta

swinging from the rafters and lying on her bed
(*Tyrannus* and *huios* grunting on top of her).

As indeed, years later, her rebellious inbred
of a daughter

would prove again, ad-libbing a gibbet
from the sturdiest stalactite on offer

(which is not to mention her betrothed,
who undid the knot of his own cricoid

with a kopis, his carotid a fury-fuelled geyser).

Il y a si peu
      entre la petite et la pénible...

Nice 'n Easy, 1999

If, occasionally, I admire my arms, my flanks,
my shoulders and buttocks against the shades,

what, before the bathroom mirror, more often
stares back, is this grotesque: soft and fault-riven.

This flesh and hair, this creased hotchpotch
of freckled fat, bulging and bobbing and blotched.

Between those strange, uncommon, fantasmatic
moments and the everyday, the chronic

shame, as each garment is yanked off or falls,
there are times like these, between your legs

(yes, like the handles of a red wheelbarrow)
where your balmy skin improves my own;

      there is *this*, our sweat-glazed *metousiosis*.

*The paintings given as titles are works by the following
artists: Paul Cézanne, Egon Schiele, Chaïm Soutine,
Clyfford Still, Frank Auerbach and John Currin*

70 (Autumn 2011)

JULIA COPUS

from Ghost

At the Farmer's Inn

Her lover lifts a Pilsner to his lips,
swallows it back
till the order arrives and they move like marionettes,
eat without talking.
Devilled kidneys, seabass, crème brûlée.

The waitresses angle their hips between tables and carry
the plates in the air,
straight-limbed as matadors. Meanwhile, the men at the bar,
afloat on their barstools,
are baying like seals; a forest of backs occludes

both the girl and her tongue-tied lover. Out of the window,
behind his head,
night falls between the slats of the trestle tables,
over the scutch-grass
and the sheep, bunched in the corner of a field.

The hubbub thickens the air like moth-wings, it beats
at the sides of her skull.
Meal over, the day's a done deal – the dawn and the dusk,
the seed, the eggs
they harvested at noon with the consummate needle,

drawing them off like tiny, luminous pearls
from the sea of her body.
Now they drink to the dregs of their coffee, call for the bill,
link hands above
the petits fours while fifty miles from here

along the unfurled ribbon of the street,
the lamplit miles
of motorway, in a clinic, a darkened room,
like mushrooms, *very*
whitely, *discreetly*, the longed-for lives begin.

Phone

She leans her head against it, listening hard,
the way the Indians in the films of her childhood
would press an ear to the ground to listen for hooves.

She's hardly slept; a little pool of violet
trembles beneath both eyes as they look out to where
a jogger has paused by the gate. The phone begins –

Good news, it says, then something she struggles to catch
and *definite signs*... The clock ticks on the wall.
The jogger passes. *Seven's a very good number*,

the voice goes on, as if it were only referring
to the lucky number of folklore and romance –
seven brides for seven beaming brothers

instead of a fragile clutch of embryos,
their fine net veils lifting in the breeze.

Inventory for a Treatment Room

Her two bare feet, six blue, translucent
overshoes that crackle
across the floodlit floor
with people

in them, one of whom's her lover;
laughter, many hushed,
expectant silences;
a stool,

white plastic, where a nurse will sit, coo-
cooing like a mother
hen, a speculum;
no windows,

no sea-breeze, but an air that hatches
occasional, tentative jokes;
a lamp on a long, extend-
able limb;

one purple treatment chair, whose empty
purple arms reach out
for her.

The Enormous Chair

Some rooms remain with us –
like this one, filled
with light enough to bleach
uncharted miles
of desert sand; a room
so impossibly bright
that once she's inside it she
can't for a moment remember
how it is she got here
or why there are nurses
padding about like kindly,
soft-footed camels;
a room with at its centre
a single chair
of the sort you might see at the dentist's
or beautician's
(except that it's purple,
except it's the size of a house,
except instead of arm-rests
there are *leg-rests*)
in whose luxurious
vinyl-cushioned depths
she's invited now to recline,
legs akimbo.

Far off, someone's stroking her left hand
very softly. Someone is calling her *sweetheart*.

71 (Spring 2012)

The Elephant Whose Sturgeon-like Blood

The elephant whose sturgeon-like blood
insists it was or ought to be aquatic,
whose ears, like hairy crackle-glazed chopping boards,
are cheerfully agreeing to be fans,
fingers his marulas with a trunk
strong enough to paralyse a tiger,
a trunk that's been wired up with special nerves
found nowhere else except the clitoris,
a trunk whose full-time job is being free
with the slightly anarchic freedom of uncertainty;
that spends its life seeing what it's like
to live as both an arm and a nose,

a trunk that never stops embracing homelessness
even while it's guiding the elephant
past the sandy smells of sons and daughters
that smell of banks of pinks and carnations
and in and out of sand-dunes and ant-hills
glittering with dew and small beetles
and down towards the water where the crocodiles
(that think they are unworthy, like Judas,
of being, of deserving to be, good)
are not as fast asleep as we think they are,
a trunk whose every nerve aspires to homelessness
even while it leads him safely home.

70 (Autumn 2011)

CRISTINA NAVAZO-EGUIA NEWTON

Edison Peña Runs the Six Miles

There are places in the Atacama desert the rain has never been to.
The rain doesn't know the inside of the puckered tunnels
in the collapsed mine where Edison Peña dreams
he's eating a fist of sand. The running scene features him
guzzling from the tap over the kitchen sink,
and his wife with washed hair reminding him there are glasses
and fondness; then a close up of himself
forever finishing that bedrock and rocksalt bite.
When he wakes up, he's still a lump in the gut of a whale
that won't cough up. A knot in the throat of a world
that swallows hard. His body is eating itself
half a mile down the driest place on earth.
Time stews slowly in the dumb tum of the mine.
Time has nowhere to go in a tumor of rock
on a spoonful of tinned fish and a sip of bad milk every other day,
and drills holes in a man that it fills with dross,
so Edison Peña gets up and runs up and down the doltish pit,
till he reckons he's done the six miles
from the mouth of the mine to the mouth of his woman
waiting at the door. Then he stops with his face to the wall.

70 (Autumn 2011)

EMILY BERRY

Zanzibar

Dear island: I blame you entirely   Your shoreline   so suspiciously   wantable
        your cunning blend of poverty and palm trees   I drew   battle lines:
your needs   versus   my needs   You won   You offered things I could not:

dolphins   oranges which are not orange   ornate doors so rare they need to be counted
    Everything I have is screwed to the ground   (the forty-five degree upside-down ground
from your angle, island)   He left behind the stuff he could not carry   or didn't want to:

    a red   corduroy armchair   an architect's portfolio   assorted ashtrays   me
When the screwed-down world turns   nothing falls but us   I spend days on my sofa
    with a crying-headache   while the skies weep on both our islands

and your drainage system is too primitive to cope   He wades   I sit at bus stops
        which seem humbler after rain   they buzz gently with a fresh   experience
London spikes up its wet hair and turns to me saying   isn't it sometimes refreshing   and

    come on   but   I imagine him   scratching mosquito bites on white beaches   being
long-limbed in new landscapes   I tramp through the definition of absence looking for a place
    to rest   island: I'm tired of thinking about your smug distant   land mass   carrying

something I want: Wicked sand-clogged island of infernal   spices   give him back

                                                                71 (Spring 2012)

SAM RIVIERE

from 81 Austerities

The Clot

I wish for the destruction of the rainforests
to continue or what would be the point
in recycling just as I wish for your
renunciation fetish to be upheld
or where is the reward in wanting
I wish my glasses were tinted 1 degree
towards dusk & noon was a touch brighter
I felt more keenly the pain of no longer
being a marxist that I didn't have
to follow girls in the galleries
of modern art but met
someone with no vaccination
scar on her bicep or I was sipping
on elemental vodka with glacial ice
or was nuzzling the sweetest intersection
of a 7-foot woman I relish a precise
anxiety when writing my wishes
I have not undertaken this
lightly and cannot
discount the
results I'm glad if
I scare easily this matches
not my desire to blaspheme with
'a new sincerity' it's not called that I
want to see clearly each thing taken from me

Dream Poem

I know what you're thinking
it's dull unless they're sex dreams
dreams about violent murders
mine are pretty banal
I dreamed I wrote a poem
beginning 'Hi!' and ending 'See You Later!'
the middle part was amazing
that's the part I don't remember
I was sitting on a platform high above the jungle
this all feels really familiar
probably from something I've seen on TV
I was dressed up as a witchdoctor
and used this stick of judgement
taking back the names of creatures
restoring them to myth I was doing wisely with it
in my dream the poem didn't have
this assonance that's creeping in
after I'd taken back everything
I kept hold of my stick using it
to designate the categories that really matter
while adding bones and wings to my hat
sitting up here out of danger
I hate this / I like that

Personal Statement

hi i should like to have the answers
to shall we say certain questions
and to wake up certain of directions
and a levelness of breathing and
of not being in a neo-noir movie
instead the mildness of the evening
and the possibility of ice-cream
waiting ahead in girlfriend heaven
when i return with gifts one chocolate
one strawberry i'll think of a question
any question the way you might prop
a stick below a window letting in
night air then pick that stick up from
its slant using it to gesture wisely
while elaborating on whatever
making all the time shall we say finer
distinctions splitting pairs of pairs
together like couples who both see
suddenly that this won't be for ever
it takes till now for the window to fall
and there can be no bitterness
or anger so what i'm saying is thank
you thank you and see you later

71 (Spring 2012)

VALÉRIE ROUZEAU

Vain Poem

The man last night who wore such classy gloves
or better than that: such glovely gloves
That man touched me with the hugeness of his eyes

Yesterday evening rain without a break his eyes
were blue were grey enormous as it rained
on his glovely sheep's-wool gloves I tell you red and gold

When when will he notice me I asked myself because
his eyes were so so big and me so close
with only a puddle between us big as a saucer big as a star

A piano was flying out of a window above our heads
a UFO if they exist that may be why
he didn't see me there while on my fingertips

a cold wet downpour pours its saucers down
on that me there. His eyes were big. The watery piano
I almost invented it through a window's light

I could see the red and gold of those winged gloves his gloves
more clearly scattering in yesterday's incessant gentle rain
the colours of the bird that dies and rises from its ash

to run run run across the piano keys
just a puddle to jump over and I could touch
instead of having nothing but two eyes to cry

Fingers of red and gold I could risk a stroke
of that soft wool the sheep the shepherdess
Oh Eiffel Tower if he were to climb

he'd see me wouldn't he Guillaume from high up there
at the puddle's edge where the round moon would flame
and I could let my fingers play as sweetly as the rain

Translated from the French by Susan Wicks

72 (Summer 2012)

SIMON ARMITAGE

The Empire

True, it wasn't the Berlin Philharmonic but it paid the rent.
McGuire served cakes and drinks on a silver tray,
made his own doilies but had to be watched with the change.
A cross-Channel swimmer, Jenkins tickled the keys in his sleep.
And I kept time on the snare: the clockwork of waltzes, foxtrots,
sometimes an eight-hour shift without missing a beat.

At night, graceful couples floated and glided wall to wall,
and never a foot out of line or a wrong move.
But the afternoons were a snake-pit of shame and sleaze:
fake shoes polished with spit and buffed with a sleeve;
charmers, chancers, carpet-baggers and bits on the side;
Altrincham widows trussed with knicker-elastic and pins…

The last straw was a wide boy in white socks
whose lady-friend squealed as his hands travelled south;
he pulled her on to his hips, then behind her back
looked me full in the face, ran his ring-finger
under his nose, breathed deep, and mouthed the word CUNT.

That was the year they lowered the great chandelier
into a wooden crate, and a mirror-ball swung in its place.
The world turned and went its thousand crazy ways.

72 (Summer 2012)

KAREN SOLIE

Spiral

i.m. J.C.

You said a storm makes a mansion of a poor man's house.
I wonder if you did so to make the best of living where
it always blew, the maddening wind that messed up our ions
and made men want to fight. Now you have no house.
There's no need. The cure took the good with the bad.

Who cannot escape his prison but must each day rebuild it?
For a year rather than drink we smoked and went to bingo.
It was like working in a mine, the air quality and incessant
coughing, bag lunches, good luck charms, the intergenerational
drama. It's not my place to say what changed.

You hadn't developed around a midpoint, and fell to the side.
A part remained exposed. Still, you were kind –
unusually so, it seems to me now, for someone with talent.
But loneliness expands to fill the void it creates. To plot against it
was to plot against yourself. You felt the effect of the whole.

When the mind is so altered this resembles death but it is
not death. Then the faint trail ran out and you continued on.
The night you've entered now has no lost wife in it, no daughter,
no friends, betrayal, or fear; it is impartial, without status.
I would like to think it peace, but suspect it isn't anything.

When our friend wrote you'd died I was on Skye,
where the wind in its many directions is directionless
and impossible to put your back to. He said you'd been living
rough for a while, he wouldn't go to the wake at the bar,
it was too much sadness. That day I'd walked the beach,

picking up shells, their spirals of Archimedes and logarithmic
spirals, principle of proportional similarity that protects
the creature and makes it beautiful. Sandpipers materialized
through tears the wind made, chasing fringes of the rising tide.
At first there were two, then three appeared, but when I began
to pay attention I realized they were everywhere.

73 (Autumn 2012)

SUSAN WICKS

Lebkuchen-Haus

She stands hunched over her stick
in the doorway, her white eyes
searching between the trees
for what? Whoever comes
is young and guileless, brittle
as matchsticks, new face painted on.

Behind her, her ginger house
is full of dark, its steep-pitched roof
iced hard. She sees the boy and girl
approaching, guards her entry-holes –
the arch of her front door's mouth,
her ox-eye window puckered like a rose.

Nothing to keep but this stale cake,
a handful of sweets fallen from the sky
and stuck to the roof like slugs
or gobs of fungus, white-tailed rats.
Yet here are six-pointed stars
in pink or yellow, her inverted heart.

Through a dust of white she sees
tree-trunks with goblin faces.
Beyond, a drift of crumbs,
a flick of feathers; that bright pane
of woodman's hut, his pile of wood,
the children on the threshold, hand in hand.

Where has her life gone
as she weighed and measured, baked
the bricks of her own house
and set them steaming on a rack in sun –
as she waited, watching for something
fragile as bird-bones, asking to be broken?

72 (Summer 2012)

TOMAŽ ŠALAMUN

Grandfather

I dreamt a huge monument, wrapping itself
with a red wire. Birds didn't peck the stone,
but the interspaces between the wires.
There were no interspaces!
The pores, my grandfather!
Your soul had always the shape of a pear.
You stood on the steep slope above the town.
You held the torch in your hands.
Townspeople started to pour each other with blood,
with the buckets.
Tacitly we went to buy an English dining room.
Everything in the room.
The portrait of young mother and
the silver chest. The salesman told us there's
another town beneath this town.
The cathedral glitters in the sun
under the earth too.
Then you fell.
You crushed the theater.
From your head people started to build
houses. Someone carried your
right thumb to his garden.
And I rushed by car on the dry river.
Your huge monument sealed the treaty.
I kept taking your stony veins from your belly and
kept testing them.
I visited your wife in the hospital
and stuffed the nurses' mouths with
five thousand dinar banknotes,
the biggest paper money then.
You were dying.
Not your wife.
Your wife died long ago,
before, in the year one thousand
nine hundred and fifty-one,
in July,
when mom cried on the terrace.

Translated from the Slovenian by
Michael Thomas Taren and the author

75 (Summer 2013)

FRANCES LEVISTON

Sulis

1.

When Sulis rose from the open ground
and entered Minerva, she mastered that shape
with such perfection she seemed to vanish
under history's golden heel,

as if Minerva sank one foot in the fountain
and poured her rival off –
only to hear in her victory-moment
a worshipper offer verbatim the prayer

Sulis drew from his mouth before,
as lovers change loved ones more than words;
only to find her eyes in the mirror
swam with someone else's tears.

2.

The gap between Senuna's teeth,
which took a thick coin or the edge of a sword,
the slit between worlds, a problem
and a wish, gushed with water day and night

into the trampled midden she ruled:
Sulis's mother, her predecessor,
recipient of plaques and the clasps of hoods,
songs and bones, the model of a lion,

who vanished after Sulis did.
There are several ways of dissolving:
to soak yourself in the baths is one;
to let the mud meet above your head is another.

3.

That owl gone hunting is the ghost
of Desdemona, or at least her after-image:
corneas domed, a dropped
hanky breast in the dark. Sulis would love her

credulous glare, the warm
mouse making its way down her gullet,
surrendering fur and ears and claws
the better to join her entourage,

and the story of how she started flying
her own feather bolster and long white ribbon,
displaced from the palace
not by a mistress, but by an avatar.

4.

Pellets indistinguishable from seed-husks
tighten round an emptiness.
Hands without another hand to hold make fists.
Under the willows

discarded vessels, void of fluid,
ache for Sulis to love them again, not leave them
there in the succulent grass.
Already she is forgetting their faces;

she leans to spit in her lover's mouth
and makes a bridge, a casual suspension
involving them both,
like spider-silk draped from cactus to cactus.

5.

Here they are, Pallas, Minerva,
with hair so heavy it bows their heads
and grey thick ankles they cool where the river
slows its rush in a kind of pond.

Nothing beyond their bodies concerns them,
nothing beyond the pools of light
their own lamps throw.
They did what they could in their time, and now

the boys who briefly rest in their shadows
cannot matter much to them,
as much as the veiled
flies on cows' faces bother the cows.

6.

Water's not particular, but where it passes is;
water like wisdom resists capture,
never complacent, revising itself
according to each new container it closes.

The heart thrives on syncresis. Sulis
hearts each man she kisses,
each costume she wears, each nakedness;
like formal dresses

she carries them with her into the cloud,
its floating parade
of people who laundered her difficult feelings
until she put them aside.

73 (Autumn 2012)

Dream Shine

When I switch off the light
The darkness lasts only
An instant, they appear

Like women in their doorways
Hesitant, brandishing
Their dim lamp. The shine

Reflected from deep snow
Edges the darkness
Of a hanging gown,

Singles out a surface,
A beam sliding upwards,
A gleam suspended;

A slice wriggles up
From a fountain in the courtyard,
Slips into the room,

Finds itself a shelf
Bobs beside it –
Who would not prefer

To sleep surrounded
By these gentle intruders,
Wrapped in their whispers?

Go to sleep, dream about
The mouse that used to watch you,
Looking out from his door

In the dashboard, obliquely,
As soon as the engine growled
And the car moved on its road.

73 (Autumn 2012)

LIZ BERRY

Bird

When I became a bird, Lord, nothing could not stop me.

The air feathered
as I knelt
by my open window for the charm –
black on gold,
last star of the dawn.

Singing, they came:
throstles, jenny wrens,
jack squalors swinging their anchors through the clouds.

My heart beat like a wing.

I shed my nightdress to the drowning arms of the dark,
my shoes to the sun's widening mouth.

Bared,
I found my bones hollowing to slender pipes,
my shoulder blades tufting down.
I spread   my flight-greedy arms
to watch my fingers jewelling like ten hummingbirds,
my feet callousing to knuckly claws.
As my lips calcified to a hooked kiss

silence

then an exultation of larks filled the clouds
and, in my mother's voice, chorused:
Tek flight, chick, goo far fer the Winter.

So I left girlhood behind me like a blue egg
and stepped off
from the window ledge.

How light I was

as they lifted me up from Wren's Nest,
bore me over the edgelands of concrete and coal.

I saw my grandmother waving up from her fode,
          looped
    the infant school and factory,

        let the zephyrs carry me   out to the coast.

Lunars I flew
              battered and tuneless

    the storms turned me insideout like a fury,
there wasn't one small part of my body didn't blart.

Until I felt it at last   the rush of squall thrilling my wing
              and I knew my voice
was no longer words but song   black upon black.

I raised my throat to the wind
              and this is what I sang...

                    Black Country–Standard English
          charm – birdsong or dawn chorus   *throstle* – thrush
            jack squalor – swallow   *fode* – yard   *blart* – cry

                        73 (Autumn 2012)

MARIA STEPANOVA

(as they must)

Night terrors
Marching their way –
Dragoons of them, tapping
Their beetle legs like twigs on dry paper.
The native population of the heart's nether-nation
Their tears cocked like a loaded weapon
Like a lesson got by rote, your words of explanation.

Once they're in, they devour everything.

And you, sweet reading
Lifting the lamp's lit arms above its head
Spreading your tent above fallen dreamers
Hiding the Jew in an empty store-cupboard.

And you, courage,
Fear's flushed veneer.
The pointless ability to rest one's cheeks in one's hands
And lift one's own head like a cup –
A cup
Barely half-filled
And quite useless:
The wine of madness, its dark contents
Spreading and taking hold in the animal body.
Oh how it foams,
Full of the dark fruits
Veiled over with a dull-blue film
Like the eye of a dying bird.

(He knows
Will he help?
Will he mix the wine with water?
Turn out the sleepless plasma screen?)

We deny, we turn away,
We walk the road step by step
Breathing with our eyes, hardly able to bear each other up,
We see acorns, fixed in the dirt clay:
Morning, morning is here!

How many of you there were, acorns.
The ones without caps,
The shaved heads of Cossacks
Burnt black in the sun,
Hardened, with long running scars.
And the ones like children, thick-walled,
Tiny barrels, big-headed boys,
So very sure of themselves
Born for the palm of the hand.

For the roll of the fist, for the life in a pocket
(A pitch dark, populous, perspiring pocket?)
In somebody's possibly kindly grasp.

You aren't for growing, for unfurling
You aren't for rupturing the paper earth,
And humming from root to topmost leaf,
Like a hive interrupted.
Nor for the extending of a ship's long deck
Or for the wearing of a feast on your back
Or for the lying as someone else's bed.
You were meant for another purpose.

The squirrel busies itself, the wind passes through
Rat-a-tat!
One by one, two by two
All they know is how to fall on the road
Where they lie, as they must.

Translated from the Russian by Sasha Dugdale

73 (Autumn 2012)

TIMOTHY DONNELLY

Apologies from the Ground Up

The staircase hasn't changed much through the centuries
I'd notice it, my own two eyes now breaking down the larger
vertical distance into many smaller distances I'll conquer
almost absently: the riser, the tread, the measure of it long

hammered into the body the way it's always been, even back
in the day when the builders of the tower Nimrod wanted
rising up into the heavens laid the first of the sun-baked bricks
down and rose. Here we are again I say but where exactly

nobody knows, that nowhere in particular humming between
one phoneme and a next, pulse jagged as airless Manhattan-
bound expresses on which I've worried years that my cohort
of passengers' fat inner monologues might manage to lurch

up into audibility at once, a general rupture from the keeping
of thoughts to oneself – statistically improbable I know but
why quarrel with the dread of it. I never counted my own voice
among the chaos, admittedly. I just figured it would happen

not with but against me. A custom punishment for thinking
myself apart from all the others. But not apart from in the sense
above but away from. Although to stand in either way will
imply nobility, power, distinction. As for example if you step

back to consider a sixteenth-century depiction of the tower
under construction, you rapidly identify the isolated figure as
that of the king, his convulsive garment the red of an insect
smitten on a calf, the hint of laughter on his face, or humming

just under the plane of his face, indicative of what you have
come to recognize in others as the kind of pleasure, no more
or less so than in yourself, that can only persist through forcing
the world into its service as it dismantles whatever happens

to oppose it, including its own short-lived impulse to adapt
by absorbing what opposes into its fabric. It will refuse to do that.
It will exhaust its fuel or logic or even combust before it lets
itself evolve into some variation on what it used to be instead

of remaining forever what it is until it dies, even when its death
comes painfully and brings humiliation down upon its house.
In the abstract, on and off – as when hurrying past the wrought-
iron fence some pink flowering branches cantilever through

or if pushed too relentlessly into oneself in public – it's hard
not to admire the resolve in that. But there are pictures in which
there is no king. The tower staggers into the cloudcover as if
inevitably, or naturally, as if the medium of earth were merely

manifesting its promise. Often the manner in which it does so
reflects the principles of advanced mathematics, but it's unclear
whether the relationship between the two might be more
appropriately thought of as one of assistance or of guidance.

This distinction is a matter of no small concern to me, actually,
because much as I don't want anyone's help, I don't want anyone
telling me what to do about ten times more, and if what it all
comes down to is that, there's a far better than average chance

I'll just end up devising some potentially disastrous third option
on the fly as I wait in line. Elsewhere we find teams of builders
at work among the tower's open spaces with no one figure leaping
forward as king or even foreman, a phenomenon whose effects

include not only the gratification of our fondness for images
of proto-democracy but also the stimulation of our need to fill
whatever we perceive to be an emptiness, which in this instance
means electing ourselves into the very position of authority

we had been happy to find vacant. I myself would be happy
leaving every position vacant as an antique prairie across which
bison once roamed democratically, each denizen of the herd
voting for what direction it wanted to take off in with a nudge

of its quarter-ton head, but someone around here has to start
taking responsibility, and I don't see any hands going up. So here goes.
Sorry. It was me. I built the Tower of Babel. What can I say?
It seemed like a good idea at the time. And a fairly obvious take-

off on what we were already doing, architecture-wise. All I did
was change the scale. I maintained the workers' enthusiasm
with rustic beer and talk of history. Plus the specter of the great
flood still freaked the people out every heavy rainfall, so it felt

like good civic planning, too – but apparently the whole project
violated the so-called natural order of things. I'm still a little shaky
with the language in the aftermath, but my gut says that's just
some dressed-up way of admitting I was really onto something.

75 (Summer 2013)

HEATHER PHILLIPSON

Oh. Is he dead?

Knee-high booties are indecorous, foot-to-face with his rabbit-like body
before the bin men have eradicated our rubbish. Dead rabbit! –
you make me a tactless stroller with my hands in my pockets, whistling.

Reality rumbles by with four fatal wheels.
Excuse the rabbit and all vegetation he offended. Touching the dead
marries them to us, us too death marries. White sheep with brown faces
are a reassurance at this time, as is a shower-proof jacket.

Your mucky side against my mucky side, dear rabbit, dead rabbit –
how similar to ours your years in random warrens, rabbiting
with your rabbit pals, going along your rabbity ways out of habit!

72 (Summer 2012)

MATTHEW ZAPRUDER

To Sergio Franchi

Listening to you sing Stella by Starlight I am thinking of the hummingbird
I actually see almost every morning hovering in the garden

I think it has a green chest but it moves too fast to really be sure
It seems to particularly love those purple flowers

Whose names no matter how many times I am told I cannot remember
Sergio Franchi I am giving in to spending a long slow hour

Holding a book closed in my lap and reading about your life
As a youth you studied both music and engineering

I imagine in those days you were not entirely happy
It makes sense later you would be so fearless

Staring into the very hot lights on the stage of the Ed Sullivan show
With effortless force pushing the air

That made the sound so beautiful and rending
My heart and I for once agree

At that moment not unlike a laundromat at night
Your light is so artificial it truly seems too real

And with a little sweat forming on your very sculptural forehead it is clear
Even you know you could never prepare us for even one long terrible afternoon

Yesterday I was walking down Stockton avoiding the many pedestrians
Crowded around the Chinese groceries with their marvelous enigmatic produce

I was feeling a little rage and also some happiness when a small grey cat
Who might or might not have been lost came up to me and with his forehead bumped my shin

Great singer, forgive me
Being myself has been a welcome unconscious chore

Today when I pass a person on the street I promise to think
You there, you could be a beautiful singer

I have carried several problems here and would like to leave them
But then who would I be

72 (Summer 2012)

D. NURKSE

Attrition

When we were children our teacher explained the war.
She drew it on the blackboard until her chalk squealed.
The dust of her erasers made us cough. What had she drawn?
Rommel's pincer movements? The oval mirror inside zero?

Our parents mimed a great massacre always,
in their weariness, their long fight over a toothbrush
clumped with white paste, their tolerance
like a series of fortified trenches. The war could return

like a stray dog and destroy us; meanwhile we were happy.
But if there were nine grapes in waxpaper in the lunchbox,
six were for the war. We could make the bombs tumble
in silence, in our minds, with no rubble.

We each had our arsenal: cap guns with a whiff of cordite
that singed our nostrils; water pistols we aimed
into our mouths, like Hitler; they tasted of piss, August pollen,
aluminum, a stray dog's anus, the last goldenrod of summer.

Then autumn and the making of the leaf fort. Then winter
and the building of the snow castle. Then spring
and the clouds massing, night and the satellites,
marriage and the deep bed, old age and the unlit lamp.

75 (Summer 2013)

JOHN McCULLOUGH

!

It entered creation as sudden as angel
or injury – the stacked letters of *io*, a tower of fire.
Already it is intimate with bishops, philosophers,
flouting borders, stowed in the peppered tails
of sentences. It infiltrates vaults, prisons,
the bedrooms of kings. I have tried to resist
but it steals from my nib, its saucy eye
rippling in candlelight, dodging pumice
and knife. Mr Smythe disapproves, names it
a feminine indulgence, the want of self-restraint.
Like Lord Allwright's secretary in greeting,
his hand travelling the road of my spine.
That tap on my rear that made verticals
govern my dreams. At night, I see vellum
with one symbol for sheet after sheet,
inscribed in blue light. My ankles vanish
and I exist, suspended, above my rounded feet.
I am always at the end of terraces, waiting
till I'm near him again, recover my form and can say
Here I am – a hot fountain in the garden
of language. The scratch of the vanquished,
those undone by the world, staring back
at the hand that shaped me, astonished.

75 (Summer 13)

poetry london
NEWSLETTER

Poems by:
Jane Duran
John Burnside
Judy Gahagan
Fred Johnston
and others

Reviews:
Docherty on Dunn +
Faber Scots
Caldwell on Paulin
Dunhill on Hill & Feinstein
Yoseloff on Boland
Truman on Celly
+ Feb Mar Listings

winter issue feb '95
volume number four
NUMBER IV

LONDON ARTS BOARD

poetry london
NEWSLETTER

JULIA CASTERTON - AMBIT - A REPLY
PASCALE PETIT ON MAD MOTHERS - HULSE & SEXTON
MONIZA ALVI TAKES PASSAGES FROM INDIA
MAURICE RIORDAN ON HUGHES O'CALLAGHAN & DOBYNS
+ POETRY FROM SHAPCOTT, KAY, WOODWARD, VALENTINE,
WILLS & OTHERS + NOTES ON ARTS FUNDING,
LATEST LONDON LISTINGS & THE RETURN OF <u>BLATHER</u>

spring issue june `92
volume number three
NUMBER II

SUBSCRIBE TO POETRY LONDON NEWSLETTER

The only publication in London to list every poetry event in the capital each quarter; plus listings of specialist libraries, workshops, evening classes borough by borough. There are articles on grant funding, resources, writing groups. What other magazine updates all the above and publishes the best in contemporary poetry and reviews. Send off 35p postage to the address below to see a back issue to judge for yourself or fill in the subscription form below.

I wish to subscribe to Poetry London Newsletter for 4 issues beginning with issue no: .... I enclose a cheque/postal order for £4.00 made payable to PLN. 26 Clacton Road, London E17 8AR.

Name...

Address..

....

....

well and has already fed poets into readings, and people from readings have come to workshops.

We want Tuesday nights and poetry and the Blue Nose Cafe to become linked in the mind of poetry London so that – even if you don't know what's on – you can come along there and feel sure that something interesting will be happening.

Amazingly, it is working! Our workshops are overflowing. Our readings are remarkably well-attended. The place has developed a feel that I like very much. All this has only been possible with the support of the Blue Nose proprietor, without whom, etc. Our programme of poetry events finishes on July 18th. But we will be restarting again in the autumn – keep an eye on listings magazines, or PLN, or come to the Blue Nose and get on our mailing list. Our sincere thanks to all those – poets and non-poets – who have supported the Blue Nose so far.'

LISTINGS

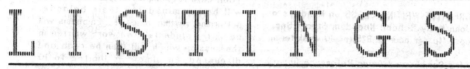

BARKING & DAGENHAM

One of the few London boroughs without a poetry group.

OTHER USEFUL CONTACTS

LIBRARY: Central library, Barking, Essex 1G11 7NE.

BARNET

NORTH LONDON WRITERS' GROUP meets once a month in member's houses around the Barnet/Finchley area. Prose and poetry are read, written by members and constructive supportive criticism is offered. Cakes and wine are usually served by the host. There is no fee. New members are welcome. Contact Jill Bamber on 883 8095

OTHER USEFUL CONTACTS

LIBRARY: Central Reference library: Ravensfield House, The Burroughs, Hendon 202 5625

THE OLD BULL ARTS CENTRE run by Pam Edwards is happy to accommodate a poetry group for the Barnet area 449 0048/ 5189. OBAC 68 High Street, Barnet, Herts EN5 5SJ.

BARNET BOROUGH ARTS COUNCIL is based at the All Saints' Arts Centre, 122 Oakleigh Road North, London N20 9EZ. (445 8388). Arts Officer Jo-Ann Hawley

BEXLEY

No poetry groups but there is the possibility of funding from the local arts council if someone wished to establish a group. Contact Mr G K Bennett, Bexley Arts Council, Hall Place, Bourne Road, Bexley, Kent DA5 1PQ. (0322 526 574)

"MIND YOU, YOU HAVE TO ADMIT THE PROFESSIONALISM OF THESE DISSIDENT POETRY GROUPS!"

OTHER USEFUL CONTACTS

LIBRARIES: Central library, Townley Road,

overkill. Neither is he much use on domestic sweetness and light, though he wants to show us he is as fond of the baby as the next man. **Sun-Gazers** is a stupefying illustration of both weaknesses in the one poem.

But this is a book to absorb for its successes. Here is an imagination as haunted and gothic as

Poe's, with a command of physical detail that makes these metaphysical parables and colloquies with the dead seem weirdly realistic. Dobyns is a poet who, in Frost's useful phrase, offers us a fresh look and a fresh listen.

Maurice Riordan

BLATHER
News, views, rumour, letters and contacts.

If you have any information for this column please write to PLN, 26 Clacton Road E17 8AR

It's all quotes this time - this little snippet came from a Hongkong newspaper/glam rag and it is quite interesting in the light of the poetry society's move:

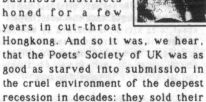

"The poets of London are no match for one who has had his business instincts honed for a few years in cut-throat Hongkong. And so it was, we hear, that the Poets' Society of UK was as good as starved into submission in the cruel environment of the deepest recession in decades: they sold their premises in a fashionable square in west London to Henry and Susan Digby. Party lover Susie was attracted by the house's spacious meeting room for musical *soirees*, etc. '**Henry was brilliant**, she told us. '**He got them down to a low enough price that we can afford to do it up.**'"

"Of twelve people in my row, three were napping, one was reading a newspaper, two were doodling." This, from James Wood's TLS account of audience involvement in the pews at an Amnesty lecture by Julia Kristeva in Oxford in March.

"**I wonder how long I'll sleep...**" George MacBeth's last words.

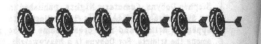

Starting Out

Editorial by *Leon Cych*

Welcome to the first issue of *Poetry London Newsletter*. PLN has been solely designed to provide a quarterly, practical outlet for advice on all the usual difficulties encountered when starting and maintaining a poetry group; it will act as a forum and bulletin board for exchange of ideas between the many groups and group members in the capital city. It will not include any poetry or criticism but the editor welcomes articles on all aspects of running a poetry group within the Greater London area.

London has a plethora of small poetry groups that meet on a regular basis and there are numerous poetry magazines, from mainstream to experimental, that are all too willing to publish their members' work, but, until now, there has been no publication which exists to bring together all these disparate organisations. Many people starting up a poetry group do not envisage the many problems that can and do occur. The perennial question about funding soon becomes one of the major obstacles. Starting up a workshop, keeping up numbers and enthusiasm of members, bringing out a magazine of their work and organizing poetry readings are the usual key areas of a small poetry group's activities.

In this first issue, *Poetry London Newsletter* will concentrate on how to get funding from Greater London Arts and in the next we will be examining the mechanics of setting up a poetry reading. Many poetry groups have a mushroom-like quality in that they seem to spring up overnight, scatter a multitude of spores to the winds and just as suddenly become overblown and fetid. This has as much to do with the nature of living in London as it has to do with the failure of any particular group to thrive and in future issues, *Poetry London Newsletter* will be featuring articles by successful group leaders who have managed to keep their groups going successfully over the years. Sadly, many small poetry anthologies fail to sell enough copies or reach enough people because, although initial enthusiasm is high on the part of group members for printing their work, this is soon dampened by the realities of having to sell and circulate copies. *Poetry London Newsletter* will be examining just how to do this in the most effective way possible. PLN is your forum so please write in!

I i (October 1988)

Blather

News, Views, Rumour, Letters and Contacts

Those avid committee members down at English Heritage (those same guardians connected with salvaging the Rose Theatre) have written back in response to our letter asking why Sylvia Plath has not yet received a Blue Plaque. Here is their reply:

Thank you for your letter of 3 June in support of the suggestion that English Heritage should erect a plaque at No 23 Fitzroy Road, Camden to commemorate the residence there of Sylvia Plath. [...] In the early part of 1988, 150 suggestions were considered by our London Advisory Committee, of which two-thirds were rejected. Among the suggestions which were not rejected however, was the one advocating the erection of a plaque to Sylvia Plath. However in view of the very great pressure on the blue plaque scheme and the relatively short period which had elapsed since Sylvia Plath's death [...] the committee considered it was reasonable to wait for a while before assessing the case for commemoration. A number of suggestions were similarly placed 'in abeyance' at that time for consideration at a future date.

Victor Belcher

I iv (September 1989)

[A plaque commemorating Sylvia Plath was unveiled in 2000 at another address in Primrose Hill. When asked why it did not mark 23 Fitzroy Road, Frieda Hughes replied: 'My mother died there... but she had lived here' (at 3 Chalcot Square). TD]

Defensible Positions

Michael Donaghy on the perfect ear of
Richard Wilbur

Every poem begins, or ought to, by a disorderly retreat to defensible positions. (Richard Wilbur)

With Faber's publication of Richard Wilbur's *New and Collected Poems* comes the opportunity to reappraise the work of that graceful lyricist, who has experienced the most widely fluctuating reputation of any living American poet. Initially he was borne aloft by the orthodoxies of postwar criticism. Through the Fifties, American poetry was supported by academic approval and most of the New Critics were themselves poets. Although these elegant craftsmen paid lip service to modernism, they were anxious to get the rough beast buried; understandably, considering the political record of the Modernists. 'Tradition' offered an escape from ideology.

Inevitably, the next generation prepared to murder its symbolic fathers. Along came Donald Allen's *The New American Poetry* and Wilbur's stock plummeted. One of the dimmer beacons of American Lit Crit, Leslie Fiedler complained that he found in Wilbur 'no personal source anywhere, as there is no passion and no insanity'. What? No insanity? This was 1964, mind you, when exhibitionism and suicide were the advisable routes to anthologized respectability and here was a perfectly sane man with the effrontery to call himself a poet!

But now, almost thirty years on, with a spirit of *détente* between the factions, it's worth considering why Wilbur never played the confessional card. He began writing poems in 1943 as a 'momentary stay against confusion', while on active service with the 36th Infantry Division. Having experienced Monte Cassino, Anzio and the Siegfried Line at first hand, he must have been rather unimpressed by the next generation's production of private hells. His decisions to eschew the confessional 'I', to write in rhyme and metre, were moral decisions, civic and militantly liberal.

During the Vietnam War, Wilbur contributed little to the available stock of protest poetry. He knew that overtly political verse is, almost always, an exercise in preaching to the converted; so he did just that. 'For the Student Strikers' begins:

> Go talk with those who are rumored to be unlike
>   you
> And whom, it is said, you are so unlike
> Stand on the stoops of their houses and tell them
>   why
> You are out on strike.

It is not one of Wilbur's best poems, but I wonder who the most profitably engaged poets of this time really were – Wilbur urging the student strikers to cultivate grassroots support for the peace movement or Robert Bly dancing about in his poncho intoning 'The Teeth Mother Naked At Last'.

But there is a final, overriding reason why a Wilbur revival is long overdue: he has a *perfect* ear, perhaps the most flawless command of musical phrase of any American poet. If only for the technique, every poet ought to own and study this book.

II ii/iii (April 1990)

Verse Design

Maurice Riordan on the New Generation promotion

I suppose all that really need be said about the New Generation promotion is that it should sell a few books, earn a couple of bob all round and possibly – just possibly – win over some long-term readers for poetry. Such presumably was the spirit in which this selection of twenty poets, all under forty or else late beginners, was put together – a rather longer list than is compatible with a real conviction that here, truly, is something new. *They are*, to recall a previous Nineties generation, *too many*.

The idea, I take it, was to jazz up the usual publicity copy, borrow a few gimmicks, turn the volume up, and lo! the media folk come to have their glasses filled. So far, this rudimentary plan seems to be working rather well: we've had the languid poses in the Sunday supplements, the glamour shots, talk of good addresses and professional careers, and much else I gather which, media-phobe that I am, I've missed. Now we may equally entertain the prospect that poets will be to the Nineties what dress designers, hairstylists and cooks (sorry, *restaurateurs*) have been to preceding decades.

Should we be cynical or purist about it all? Cynical: to be sure. But purist? I think not. Poets, once they've done their best for a poem, still have the job of getting it out, beyond the perimeter of private admiration and the watchtowers of punditry, into the world of its potential readers. It can be an unwholesome business and opportunism and coat trailing are not totally unknown among the secondary talents of poets. So, at least for this twenty, the business is done; they can have little excuse henceforth if their work is ignored or forgotten.

Storms of publicity, then, are to be embraced. But storms pass, and your poems enter calmer waters, make their way indeed for the most part in utter tranquillity. They survive – if they do survive – by stealth, revived by those library-bound or late-night quiet collisions with susceptible minds. Even as I write my hand strays, irrelevantly, to the bookshelves to read over half-remembered lines by E.A. Robinson, Thomas McCarthy, Landor: poets, as it happens, not currently on too many lists. It is the kind of foraging everyone reading this is familiar with. Random, seemingly inconsequential, mysterious, it is, I'd suggest, the unremarkable means by which a literary culture is maintained, strengthened and renewed. And I hope, in the midst of all the hoopla, no-one's entirely lost sight of the process. It beats me the alacrity with which people hitch poetry to latest trends, the enthusiasm with which they want to confuse poems with rock, rap, video or whatever. Sure we'd like some of the mass attention given to them; but do we want the span of attention given to them as well?

It would be churlish, in this context, to pick and choose among the books selected for promotion. A few, as it seems to me, are already on their way to that sure oblivion from which the best efforts of Colman Getty PR won't detain them long. But most are books I'd want on my shelves available for that random foraging by which poems get sorted over time. There is undoubtedly a whiff of the new here (though fainter than hype can allow): a shift from cleverness to intelligence, a confidence with big ideas, and above all, a sense that language is fully available. Many would cite Elizabeth Bishop as an influence and her self-effacing, yet venturesome curiosity may well offer poets a good approach to the sort of open-ended future we now find before us. For, make no mistake, a clear hole has appeared in the canopy, and all poets, on the list or not, should be making for it. Not the limelight, but the real light! Risk, speculative energy, a sense of adventure – these are what it's going to be about. The great turn-of-the-century poems are there to be written: which, if any, of these poets write them remains to be seen.

IV ii (May 1994)

Poetry London Newsletter Enters the Digital Age

Editorial by *Leon Cych*

This issue is a little later than normal because we have been testing *e-mail* facilities and *Web* pages for use on the Internet. We are proud to announce that we are the first poetry magazine in southern England on the Internet with a *World Wide Web* page. On Burns night we posted Brian Docherty's article to several specialist Usenet groups on the Internet (it is estimated as many as sixty thousand people read these groups) and received a large number of welcoming and supportive *e-mail* replies – several universities in the United States now have this document in their archives.

The power of such a resource can be seen [...] by accessing our new *World Wide Web* page (see back cover). If none of this makes sense to you, visit Marylebone Library or the Cyberia Café in Whitfield Street [...] to see what we're talking about, and when you're there, ask someone to type in [the] address of our poetry page – you'll soon see what poetry resources are out there and what an amazing resource the Internet is.

IV iv (May 1995)

A Good Thing

Mimi Khalvati can't get enough of workshops

My life in workshops (for such it is) has gone through several phases:
1. the toe in the water phase
2. the going manic phase
3. the getting pissed off phase
4. the 'a little of a good thing' phase
5. the DIY phase

To expound:

My 'toe in the water phase' turned out to be more than a toe and definitely a good thing. Camden Voices, run by Dinah Livingstone for nearly twenty years, has helped many people, including me, to find their feet. Up to 1990, it ran as an ILEA class and has now transferred to the Working Men's College. I went to Dinah's class for several years, loved going, learned a lot and wrote a lot of poems that I learned, slowly and reluctantly, were totally obscure to everyone but me (and perhaps one other obscure would-be poet). Obscurity is not a good thing. Difficulty is something else, but it's hard to know which is which. I also learned about 'The Ear'. The Ear, a Good Ear, is a good thing.

The 'Going manic phase' meant going to about four workshops a week, sometimes workshopping the same poem several times to end up none the wiser. Getting a feel for 'the scene', with similar results. When you weren't workshopping, you were going to readings; and when you weren't going to readings, you were reading the poets whose readings you did or didn't get to and when you... you had to write the bloody poems. Blue Nose poets were (still are) a good thing. And were good to me. Torriano was (still is) great and gave me my first reading with Jane Duran, my DIY other half.

The 'Getting pissed off phase'. Well, who wouldn't? Hearing the same thing over and over again: cut, cut, cut. The poem, the sentence, the beginning, ending, but most of all the sentence, whose head was in the second verse – the one you were supposed to cut. Limbs, one cut off at a line ending so how were they supposed to understand that? The fingers, splayed out over lines eleven, twelve, thirteen, thirteen-and-a-half (I'm beginning to sound like Adrian Mole) belonged to the wrist, not the elbow which was way down in the penultimate verse – the one everyone liked so that was OK. The limbs, as I was saying, spread over pages three to four and as for those toes... you get my drift. Another piss-off was The Abstract. No ideas but in things. No ideas, only things. Don't tell, show. Don't think, feel. Ground rules are fine. Reacting against Victorian verse, the worst excesses of, is fine *if*... if you haven't been doing it for the last eighty years. Personally, I'm reacting against the worst excesses of my own times as I see it, them, and that's one good reason for going to workshops – to see them.

The 'A little of a good thing phase'. Usually in private. Private workshops you get invited to, or wangle your way into, or set up your own and let them do the wangling. The N7 Workshop set up by Myra Schneider, Colin Rowbotham and Caroline Price is a good thing. The best thing about it is the set-up, the structure. Structure makes all the difference. To people. They change. According to the structure. No more jumping on the bandwagon. No more long and heated discourses on that comma, that adjective the first person who opened their mouth went on about and everyone followed suit and that took care of your precious ten minutes. No more poems crying 'No-one understands me', in the corner. Or struggling to be fully born when all they want is a post-mortem. Picking over remnants. How about this bit, that bit? That line's great, keep it!

The 'DIY phase' meant, over a year ago, setting up all-day workshops on the first and third Saturday of every month with Jane Duran who's in the States at the moment so she can't vet this or help me write it, for that matter, or make me rewrite it. These originated at the Torriano Meeting House, thanks to John Rety and Susan Johns's generosity and hard work.

We're now also running last Saturday workshops at The Poetry Society and Pascale Petit is running second Saturday workshops in Walthamstow. That takes care of Saturdays. I'm also starting a Versification Course at The Poetry Society this autumn for the hordes out there who want to do more technical stuff. Me included.

I was asked to do a chatty piece. An out-and-about in London piece. A workshop piece. I'm neither chatty nor out-and-about much except to and from workshops. But I am a list person, so I'll list a few reasons why workshops can be a good thing:

- workshops create readers
- writing's lonely and workshops can give you a sense of community, family even, offer friendships, collaborations and, as I've found at the Goldsmiths College poetry workshop, can introduce you to parts of London other workshops haven't reached
- workshops teach ground rules which – as long as they don't become dogmatically prescriptive – are a good thing
- workshops can specialize and meet particular needs – witness the spectacular success of Survivors' Poetry
- workshops can be playful and writers need to be
- workshops create readers and critics – the ones inside your head who can, through your eyes, read your work in progress, cut it, develop it, admire it, bin it. Do what you'd do for others. In other words, help you to define your ideal reader, become your own best critic
- workshops help you define your context and how you see it, where you stand vis-à-vis it and what then, are the prizes and penalties
- a whole lot more besides – writing exercises, experiment, technique, confidence, humility, publication, performance. The list is endless but I want to end with a quote from Tillie Olsen: 'A poet's inspiration has to illuminate the forest, not set fire to a single tree' (and she's not talking rainforests).

Workshops can also be a bad thing. If they don't do all or some of the good things or overdo them so that friendly becomes cliquey, non-elitist becomes philistine, affirming breeds complacency and everything gets back-to-front… which in itself is not necessarily a bad thing.

25 (Autumn 1996)

[The Saturday workshops Mimi Khalvati mentions were to grow into the Poetry School, founded in 1997 with the aim of providing structured, high quality teaching programmes for adults and now a national organisation specialising in teaching poetry. For many years *Poetry London* and the Poetry School shared office accommodation. TD]

Guided by Voices

Paul Farley doesn't know whether he's coming or going

Funny thing, *Carte Blanche*. Write something about anything was the dream ticket I supposed all cub writers hoped for when they were given a word count and deadline. How wrong can you be? Faced with the winking cursor and blank screen, I'm left thinking of the 'open mike' – all manner of currents and stirrings run through my formative experiences of this ordeal, for ordeal it was. Something happens when you decide one day that this is something you must do. Read your poems out loud. To other people. Strangers. For me, it immediately threw into relief some schism lying dormant since my teens, a kind of conflict of the head and the heart. It goes something like this – do I want these words to avoid beauty and harmony, to exude conflict and unresolved tensions; or do I want to get a laugh? For once, something cultivated largely in total privacy is going to be aired, and might be found wanting. Why am I doing this?

The smart-arses amongst you are probably mumbling 'integrity' and 'truth to original vision' around about now (the idiots will be thinking 'money'). I'd contest that this is wisdom way after the event in most cases. The first reading I gave, in a cliché of a darkened room above a pub, quickly brought my head up to speed with my heart. I remember several things happening before – clocking the pamphlets fanned by the petty cash-box, my name being added to the bottom of a sad little list, being told that I couldn't smoke – then it being over, and a smattering of applause, and the indelible sense that I would write in a certain way from that point on, neither to please a crowd or flatter an ego, but because it was the only way that satisfied emotional *and* intellectual imperatives. I think I came to some decision about rejecting the textual shenanigans that had preoccupied me for a while, reading the poems out loud, though I have since seen readers exploit such effects brilliantly (sometimes I *lean over to one side* during italicized passages). Opening their gobs simply forces people to bolster or chuck out things.

It'll be apparent by now that I've a predilection for this spoken word business, probably because I'm aware of my own accent and the sense of difference that it can engender. It's fundamental stuff; but sometimes obscured or forgotten by various smarty pants – all the social and cultural bric-a-brac of one's life trying to preserve their sound and rhythms, while at the same time needing to make themselves heard. Anybody with any kind of accent must have felt this, providing they got past that wonky deal table with the books on by the door.

The speaking voice and the mind's can seem to disengage alarmingly over time, like that sight gag where the trailer glides past the car that was towing it – my voice, to anyone who's listening, is basically textbook Scouse (what textbook? try *Does Accent Matter?* by John Honey) but the voice in my head, the voice equally able to intone phrases, sentences and pick over the sound and weight of words, seems to be an amalgam of early reading and of a mediated RP I've picked up in my childhood, what Heaney calls 'the absolute speaker'. Weird. Trying to square these two and the concomitant traffic between them seems to be where the poetry resides, though of course every time I consciously go knocking, there's nobody home. I seem to have written a short treatise on how we are shaped and formed sometimes despite ourselves. Give some people six hundred words and they're anybody's.

28 (Autumn 1997)

May I Make a Suggestion?

Michael Donaghy comes up with five rules for the newly enrolled poet

Students sometimes enroll in poetry classes in order to learn what they take to be a set of formal rules for writing verse, so in my workshops I'm at pains to emphasize that there are no rules for writing poetry. Or rather that there are innumerable sets of unforeseeable rules; imagine a form of chess incorporating all the known manoeuvres with their infinite permutations but add as legitimate moves licking all the chess pieces one by one or scattering petals on the chessboard or slapping your opponent with a rubber chicken.

Welcome, I say, this is a workshop for poets of all levels. Are you a genius? I ask them. If so, please stay at home and write your opus. You don't go to the doctors to show how fit you are. You don't take your car to the garage so the mechanics can admire it. You don't take a poem to a workshop if you don't want advice.

Over the years I've noticed that good poetry is thoroughly unpredictable. It always surprises. But bad poetry is always bad in the same way. So I've collected a set of suggestions, which I advise the inexperienced to follow for six months. After that, I tell them, drop them and follow your instinct.

1. **Read it...** Literature is a conversation. You have to know what and how poets are writing before you enter that dialogue. Imagine a musician who doesn't listen to music or a dinner guest who insists on talking while refusing to listen. Bad poetry is not unrelated to bad manners. Collect poems that move you and read them carefully. Poets dream of exerting an influence on other writers. It's only polite to steal everything you can.

2. **Say it...** Don't be 'unspeakable'. That is, use ordinary word order – the kind of sentences one would use when speaking to be understood. Test your poem by speaking it aloud and write as if you're actually speaking to someone.

Don't, for example, distort the normal word order to force a rhyme or sound unspeakably 'poetic', as in 'He drew his sword the scabbard from' or 'Down the boulevard I did stroll'. This gives your writing an affected antiquity – rather like wearing a monocle. Similarly, avoid using unspeakably 'modern' sentence fragments; 'whistlestream brownpour contentsigh' is not a daring way of describing a cup of tea. It's just silly.

3. **Show it...** Whenever you want to say something, stop. Don't. Show it instead. The sad fact is no-one wants to know what you think. They want to discover what they think. If you show what you mean through concrete imagery, readers will discover meaning for themselves. An idea is more effectively communicated if you can see, touch, hear, smell or taste it. A colt kicking and bucking in a frosty paddock before dawn, the newsagent opening his shop, looking up into the sun and bursting into an out-of-tune rendition of Bizet's 'March of the Toreadors' – the word 'joy' is a vague and inadequate way to label these specific instances.

4. **Listen...** What makes a person a bore in conversation? Droning on about himself? Or about people you don't know? Preaching? Telling you what to think? All these things make for boring poetry too. So listen to yourself and consider the impatient reader. More importantly, listen to the poem you're writing. If you've made up your mind what you're going to say and stick to it whatever the surprise the writing has in store for you, you're practising the art of advertising.

5. **Shape it...** I use the term 'integritas' to describe a synthesis – the way in which a poem is established as all one thing – a term I've borrowed from James Joyce:

> In order to see that basket, said Stephen, your mind first of all separates the basket from the rest of the visible universe which is not the basket. The first phase of apprehension is a bounding line drawn about the object to be apprehended... That is integritas.

'Integritas' is the first step to what Joyce calls 'radiance'. When you play with the boundaries of the poem, you exploit an irresistible human instinct: just as we stare ink blots in a Rorschach test into the shape of clouds, or people, or animals, we long to wrest coherence from the structure of a poem. The reader is willing to go halfway to accommodate you – but no more.

31 (Autumn 1998)

A Few Changes
Editorial by *Peter Daniels*

New office, adjusted title, new website... None of it much to do with poetry in itself, but the aim is to keep poetry flowing, by finding enough space and a suitable presence; working from rooms in several flats and houses hasn't been easy. The active and expanding Poetry School has been in the same situation, and together we've found a lovely office at the Quaker meeting house in Walthamstow. It started life as a printing works, which feels appropriate, though I don't suppose they produced much poetry. Walthamstow is bustling, but it isn't Covent Garden; and the overall feeling is peaceful and spacious, with a sweeping view towards – well, suburban Chingford. This isn't Waterloo Bridge, either.

While we've found a home in real space, we're getting properly out there in the virtual world with our new website. Does the internet make the city redundant? Is there any reason why *Poetry London* rather than *Poetry Spitzbergen* or *Poetry Timbuktu*? It's a matter of identity really. Maybe you're sitting in the daisies on the edge of a cliff with a laptop; we're at the end of the Victoria Line in a conglomeration of people who mostly 'come from' elsewhere (however you define that). People want to get together in cities, and despite the efforts of crazed ethnic cleansers with bombs, we feel it's worth it.

Virtual and real sites have their own virtues, their own realities; you don't have to access a computer to be part of London, and you don't have to come to London to read or contribute to our magazine.

So here we are – wherever 'here' is.

33 (Summer 1999)

'It's About Language and How it Works'

John Stammers interviews *Jo Shapcott*, winner of the Forward Prize for *My Life Asleep*

STAMMERS: The new compendium of your work, *Her Book*, contains the poem 'Muse', which makes the muse explicit for once. Does this poem represent what you think it really is?

SHAPCOTT: I think that a muse figure, or an inspiration source, is a shifting thing for everyone. That poem was taking the angle that the female muse is very tractable and kind to those whom she inspires. Those of us who are stuck with a male muse have someone much more stubborn, uncooperative and unwilling – maybe even competitive. So the poem represents an encounter between the speaker and that kind of muse.

STAMMERS: So, do you feel yourself stuck with a male muse?

SHAPCOTT: I think that the muse is a shifting quality. All I can tell you is that it usually is. Drat!

STAMMERS: You'd prefer a female muse?

SHAPCOTT: It's a feminist poem. What it proposes is that it's harder, for all sorts of historical reasons, to do with gender and the tradition. There aren't enough models of women writing poetry, so when we encounter the tradition we have to find a way to completely engage with what's gone before, a way to possess it. This is the case, even though what's happening inside, say, a Sidney poem, is not the same dynamic as would happen to you as an individual because of the gender difference. So there's a way to lay claim to that by acknowledging what the difference might be. Sidney made play with the convention against a notion of truth. That's what I would seek to do in a modern context. You will notice that at the end of the poem she has to silence the muse.

STAMMERS: I also want to invite you to discuss the place of science in your work. This realm, stereotypically a male one, seems to be a field of exploration for you.

SHAPCOTT: I believe that poetry can encounter anything – that it can go anywhere. Perhaps it's even more important, now that electronic media can take us off anywhere, that poetry can take you further still, imaginatively. I think that's more acute for a woman because for ages there have been areas of writing that have been seen as women's, and it's good to feel that that is no longer so.

The other aspect is language. I'm suspicious of poems about science. I suppose I'm suspicious of poems 'about' anything. I think in my poems you'll see explorations of different languages. Yes, you'll see poems like 'Quark', which really move into science with a lot of joy and discovery, but it's not about science, it's about language and how it works. I think that languages spring up anywhere that someone has a passion or interest – a whole language that becomes tribal and almost as local or district-based as a dialect.

STAMMERS: *Her Book* contains most of your work. It doesn't contain, however, the versions of the Rilke Rose poems. Recently we've seen *The Eyes* by Don Paterson – a version of Machado that got a lot of attention, particularly regarding the status of the poems. As someone who has written versions, what do you think about that?

SHAPCOTT: I've been working on Rilke's poems in French for almost ten years. Rilke wrote over three hundred poems in French; they're really rather gorgeous. The metaphysical depth, however, is still there. It has taken a long time because it's been a project I've kept by me to turn to when I didn't want to write my own poems or when my own poems weren't coming. The straightforward translations I started off doing were not good poems. I began to lean towards my responsibility to make good poems and because of that, to get more interested in Rilke and more keen, almost, to talk to him directly. Don't you always find this urge towards the writers who absorb you, who become influences?

Rilke became like that for me, particularly the twenty-seven-poem sequence 'The Roses'. My poems are probably not versions, they are conversations. In some cases they even say 'it's not like that, it's like this'. So, although they relate strongly to the originals, in some cases they may in fact have the opposite sense, as part of the argument. The roses, I began to realize, were probably twenty-seven girl-friends, or maybe even twenty-seven different sets of female genitalia. Because his image range is so confined – petal, space, petal – it's extraordinary that each one is so different. He addresses the rose in each of these poems: 'O Rose you are like this, O rose you are like that'. In mine, however, I very quickly let the rose herself have a voice so it becomes the first person; they answer him. Both sequences are also extended love poems. I began to see that mine is probably a love poem to Rilke himself.

STAMMERS: You have co-edited two anthologies, *Emergency Kit* with Matthew Sweeney, and *Last Words* with Don Paterson. I wonder if you'd say something about the editing process.

SHAPCOTT: *Emergency Kit* took three years to put together. Matthew and I worked very hard at it. We did aim it at a certain type of person. We imagined someone who was perhaps interested in poetry but didn't know very much yet. We hoped they could be enthused if they knew the range and the excitement they could find there. We both came to it with a stash of poems that we knew could have that magic effect. But we also did lots of reading. This was because the parameters of the book were broad – it was world-wide poetry first written in English. I must say, and

I'm allowed to say this because it's not my poetry, I still love that book, still enjoy it and feel glad when I see it. I also think it was a good antidote to a lot of the summing up anthologies! You know: who's in, who's out; it's a more open book than that.

STAMMERS: What I find interesting is that the poems have a special quality. There are, for example, some very good poems, which would not fit in that. I wonder how you arrived at that approach.

SHAPCOTT: I'm glad you picked up on that quality. I think it was exactly what we were aiming at. We might have a quite strange poem from someone's work, but which fits. It's those poems where you sense the poet has discovered something en route through the process of writing. You certainly know that when you read it. The other anthology that I co-edited, *Last Words*, was extraordinarily different. It was made up of specially commissioned poems. So the editorial function was to persuade poets they should contribute, then pretty much accept what they contributed. Although that book, I think, gives a real snapshot of what about a hundred poets were doing in the last months of the last century.

STAMMERS: The final poem in *Her Book* is about, and to, the writer, Dennis Potter. What influence do you think he had on you and in what way?

SHAPCOTT: Dennis Potter came from the Forest of Dean: a weird little area in the west of England on the Welsh border. It's a mining area, or used to be, and dirt poor – still is, really, in pockets. My family come from there and were a mining family. So, whenever I heard Dennis Potter speak on radio or on television, just his accent and his dialect flicked me back to my own parents. It could be just using a simple word like 'lass', which my dad used to call me, or broader dialect like 'Ow bist old butt?' which means 'How are you old friend?'. So, it would true to say there was a lot I admired about him as a playwright – it's Forest of Dean magic realism meeting post-war leftist politics.

I also liked his politics and the fact that he was one of our last ranters. People are not so bold now about shouting against injustice or bureaucracy or political hypocrisy. He was problematic, though, and I think that began to interest me: given the nature of the tradition, yet again I am in the position of trying to mediate with a literary father. This is particularly true given that Potter's own attitude to women was so muddled, so destructive for him and probably others. I never met him, but after he died I wrote him the letter that is the poem. Which must be the only poem in the language to contain a singing penis!

STAMMERS: So what can we look forward to from you in the near future?

SHAPCOTT: *Tender Taxes*, my next book, is out Spring 2001. It is a whole book of versions of Rilke's French poems. It'll include, along with other poems, the 'Roses' sequence from *My Life Asleep* and the 'Windows' sequence from *Phrase Book*.

36 (Summer 2000)

Emulating Scarlatti's Sonatas

August Kleinzahler on his mentor, *Basil Bunting*

Basil Bunting described himself as a 'minor poet, not conspicuously dishonest'. With this handsome, authoritative, two-hundred-and-forty-four-page edition of his *Complete Poems*, readers will be able to judge for themselves where Bunting stands among twentieth-century poets writing in English. I envy a young reader coming upon Bunting's poetry for the first time and engaging the work with an open, attentive mind. Bunting wrote that his poetry was written for the pleasure of 'unabashed boys and girls'. Well, they can be as unabashed as they like, but they had also better be determined, astute readers. And if their range of taste and prior reading is limited to the fashionable poets of the moment, they had best be prepared for some arduous, perhaps uncomfortable, stretching.

Let me make some general observations for the reader coming fresh to these poems and this collec-

tion. The actual *Collected Poems*, that work which Bunting chose (shortly before his death) to remain in print, amounts to a mere hundred and forty-three pages. And on many of these pages there is a good deal of white space. The *Collected* includes six long poems, what Bunting called Sonatas, the earliest, 'Villon', dating from 1925. The last, 'Briggflatts', his masterwork, was completed in 1965. There are two books of 'odes', short poems usually of a page or less in length, the First Book containing thirty-nine odes, the earliest from 1924, the last from 1939. 'The Second Book of Odes' contains twelve poems, extending from 1954 to 1980. The *Collected* includes an extended adaptation into English (made from an Italian translation) of a work by the Japanese writer, Kamo-no-Chomei (1124–1216), entitled 'Chomei at Toyama'.

Finally, the *Collected* includes thirteen of what Bunting called 'overdrafts', which are to be regarded as loose translations, almost exclusively from Latin and Persian originals. And that's it. Why so little? I don't believe it is; and one might fairly ask why so many recent poets publish so bloody much. In brief, Bunting had an erratic, eventful, often difficult life. He was not a university man. Through much of his life he lived hand to mouth and in circumstances that made the writing of poetry difficult, if not impossible. At the same time, he was rigorous in his refusal to duplicate what had been done before, either by others or by himself. If he had nothing to offer of real poetic value, he gave forth nothing. Which may serve as a salutary model for some of the more self-regarding and unabashed gushers at work out there presently.

The difficulties of Bunting's poetry are considerable. Let me mention only three kinds. Ezra Pound, Bunting's mentor in many things, quotes Bunting's phrase 'DICHTEN = CONDENSARE', in the *ABC of Reading*. Bunting's poetry is exceedingly dense, its syntax scrambled (at least in relation to conventional usage), and is stripped down as far as it can be, with an uncommon, and really quite extreme, dearth of connectives. You'll be hard-pressed to find too many relative pronouns in those hundred and forty-three pages of the *Collected*. The poetry is paratactic, elliptical, and wound very tightly indeed. So tightly, that even the most practiced reader will have difficulty, here and there, in unravelling it.

The poetry is often allusive, and these allusions can at times be deliberately obscure or exotic, arising from Bunting's broad knowledge of foreign literature, along with his wide travels and multifarious experience. Insofar as he is a modernist in the tradition of Pound and Eliot, Bunting doesn't hesitate to court difficulty, on occasion, one might argue, for its own sake. Finally, I would point out to the new reader that Bunting exhibits in his work a uniquely developed attention to patterning and structure. Among his models was the baroque sonata form, most especially that of Domenico Scarlatti, about whom Bunting writes in 'Briggflatts':

It is time to consider how Domenico Scarlatti
condensed so much music into so few bars
with never a crabbed turn or congested cadence,
never a boast or a see here...

There are fugal elements at work in all the long poems as well, most especially 'Briggflatts', with a central motif and different lines added along the way that comment upon and embroider that motif. The Lindisfarne illuminated manuscripts were a central influence, as would have been the patterning and ornamentation he encountered elsewhere in other arts and cultures, not least among them the Near Eastern. The reader may be assured a design is at work in any given poem, no matter how brief, and it will often be disguised or hidden, asking to be tricked out.

The patterning, however, is not restricted to the architecture of the poem, but is most in evidence through the organization of consonants and vowels, stressed and unstressed syllables. Bunting is the most satisfyingly musical poet among moderns, Pound included, and to properly appreciate his achievement, these poems have to be sounded out by the reader, so they are literally tasted in the mouth:

It sounds right, spoken on the ridge
between marine olives and hillside
blue figs, under the breeze fresh
with pollen of Apennine sage.

It feels soft, weed thick in the cave
and the smooth wet riddance of Antonietta's
bathing suit, mouth ajar for
submarine Amalfitan kisses.   ('Briggflatts')

Bunting himself would have the reader simply enjoy the poetry as an aural experience, however dense with meaning and detail the poetry may otherwise be. He felt that the meaning of a poem inheres in the sound, whether or not you can follow the 'sense' of what is happening. And this is how the new reader should at first engage the poetry, not worrying about the allusions and design, or even what the damn thing is about.

But however much of the sound you are able to get on your own, nothing can match the master himself reading these poems aloud. I recall the first time I heard Bunting read aloud to a large audience in 1971, it nearly took the top of my head off, and I actually had a serious headache for days afterwards. It is with especial delight that I can report that the good people at Bloodaxe, in conjunction with Richard Caddel, director of the Bunting archive in Durham, have made available a two-cassette package of Bunting reading his poetry aloud in both studio and live settings, including the great, and nearly impossible to find, 1967 Stream recording of 'Briggflatts'. Bunting's greatest poetry came relatively late in life. The degree of growth from his early work, heavily influenced by Pound and Eliot, is extraordinary. There is no longer any doubt, unless among hard-core cranks, about the unparalleled achievement of 'Briggflatts'. If Bunting was indeed a protégé of Pound, then this is the flower of that poetic vision or set of methods, a hard, spiky northern flower, and a poem finally that Pound, in thrall to his various masks and lacking in both experience and humanity, didn't have in him.

But there is much, much more on offer in this collection than 'Briggflatts', and even without that masterpiece these other poems of Bunting's would establish him as a major, not a minor figure in the poetry of this past century. If you are interested in checking how good Bunting was how young, then have a good, hard look at 'Ode No. 3' in 'The First Book of Odes', written in 1926. It is a love poem and a corker – Bunting is, above and beyond anything else, a love poet. Read it through once aloud, then have a look again; there's an abab rhyme in place that is so subtly handled, that, if you're like me, you may have entirely missed it the first time through.

There are scores of other such pleasures, both early and late, and I haven't the space here to tell you a small fraction of them. You will find them on your own. As for the *Uncollected Poems*, well, there was probably good reason Bunting didn't want them reprinted, but among them is some magnificent poetry, most especially 'A Song for Rustam', written upon the death of a young son he had never seen. One poem that didn't make it into his *Collected* that he did want to see published (as a children's book) is the marvellous adaptation of the Persian children's poem, 'The Pious Cat', in which Bunting takes not a few liberties. Here Bunting describes some of the goodies the grateful mice have brought their own 'Saint Tibbald' on the occasion of the cat who

> '... has been converted!
> He has turned charitable and meek
> and means to fast six days a week,
> and on the seventh he will eat
> acorns and trash instead of mouse meat'.
> So all the mice cried: 'Halleluia!
> You don't suppose he'll relapse though, do ye?'
>
> To give their gratitude a vent
> seven eminent mice were sent
> to take Saint Tibbald a testimonial.
> They marched with dignified ceremonial
> and every mouse of them had brought
> gifts of the most expensive sort.
> The first mouse brought a bottle of Schiedam
> The second brought a roast leg of lamb.
> The third mouse brought a red currant tart;
> the fourth, spaghetti by the yard;
> the fifth, hot dogs with Cocacola.
> The sixth brought bread and gorgonzola.

And so on. My, what parties mice gave in medieval Persia! We are most fortunate to have Bunting's poems in print once again, and it seems that at long last the poet is beginning to be afforded some of the attention this work deserves, not least of all in his native England. What remains to be done is for Bloodaxe, or whoever else is interested, to publish a collection of Bunting's prose writings and interviews, which, you will probably not be too terribly surprised to learn, make fascinating reading and should make an excellent complement to the poems.

37 (Autumn 2000)

Video Installation Poetry

Editorial by *Pascale Petit*

There's a frozen head cast in the artist's own blood, his features fading under ever-thickening crusts of maroon ice. Next door, in a huge glass cabinet, bluebottles hatch, feed on a rotting cow's head, then are insect-o-cutored. And here's the room closed to unaccompanied under-eighteens, where Jake and Dinos Chapman have created 'Zygotic acceleration' – a ring of fused children bearing genitalized faces.

I'd encountered most of these works before their Royal Academy debut, but it was the respectable venue that drew the public in droves to see our Young British Artists. It was as if Faber had published an anthology of radical and sensational new poetry. And it left this editor wondering: where is the *Sensation* show of British poetry? Bloodaxe with its 'edge' and 'new blood' might aspire to it. Anvil's *Beyond Bedlam* was at least uncomfortable in its subject matter. But the question arises – compared to the visual arts, is contemporary British poetry conservative?

When I started co-editing this magazine back in 1990, I was still an artist. My transition into the poetry world included a crash course in social etiquette and middle-class mores – no-one had bothered with all that at art school. In the studio, it was perfectly acceptable to be rude! While I'm not suggesting poets should be rude to each other, I do propose that politeness inhibits art. Neither am I suggesting that poets must use shocking subject matter – a good poem should shock with its fresh language and imagery. Artists may have new media: video installation, neon, Nasa refrigeration units, but poets have the ever-evolving, heterogeneous English language, freighted with all its exotic vocabularies from science, technology, and diverse cultures. And poets are image-makers. They can create durable and haunting icons of our age with words – they don't have to struggle with unwieldy stuff. Yet, it's to an artist that I turn for one of the most haunting images of our time.

The setting is Durham Cathedral. A large screen has been installed over the Great West Door. A luminous dot grows in the centre. Slowly I realize it's a man surfacing from the sea, his illuminated gold body breaks through the blue water to deliver a message: to exhale a single long held breath, shattering the silence. After a few moments, he inhales deeply, and sinks back into the dark. The cycle then begins anew. The effect is primal in its forcefulness, creating arguably one of today's most poetic artworks. Interestingly, Bill Viola's 'The Messenger' was inspired by lines of Walt Whitman, and Viola is an American. But there are European artists whose work is lyrically poetic – Mona Hatoum, Cornelia Parker, Rebecca Horn, to name a few. Much of 'The Messenger''s power lies in its singularity – one kinaesthetic event is composed with colour, light, time and sound. The best poets order their images with comparable concentration and care. Whether they innovate with traditional forms, like a painter finding new ways to paint with oils on canvas, or whether they stretch language and images towards the verbal equivalent of video installation art, poets must take risks. Even if these fail, poets must go beyond gentility and convention, experiment with form and content, if poetry is not to fall behind and remain ignored by a broader public.

39 (Summer 2001)

Hidden Abysses of Feeling

D.M. Black on *Pascale Petit*'s *The Zoo Father*

Funny things happen to fathers when they die and get turned into poetry. Shakespeare in *The Tempest*, in one of his most surreal moments, describes the drowned father of Ferdinand: 'Of his bones are coral made; Those are pearls that were his eyes...' And when Macbeth describes the butchered fatherly king Duncan, somehow we are unsurprised that the appalling gore has been turned into heraldry: 'his silver skin', says his murderer, was 'laced with his golden blood'. It's hard to account for the success of these transformations, but it has, I think, something to do with the enormous kindness of Shakespeare's own vision. The father is beyond doing good or evil, and whatever his actual life was like, he can now become an object of unconditional love.

Pascale Petit is working in a very different way. Most of the poems in *The Zoo Father* are about her actual father, and we are told fragments of a family history, tantalizing and incomplete as family histories always are. The father is described as raping the mother, repeatedly, and Petit believes herself to be the child of a rape. There was also a younger brother, and both children were sexually abused in some way, never made fully clear, by the father. When Petit was eight, her father abandoned the family and they moved from Paris to Wales. Many years later, dying of emphysema, the father recontacted his daughter, and she went to be with this almost unknown man while he was dying. Much of this book was written during this period, and the poems portray with savagery and wit, and sometimes a sort of unnerving relish, the hugely complex emotions of the adult woman she had now become. Petit writes as someone still affected by her history, but also able to understand, as a fellow adult, something of what may have been going on for her parents while they were together in their tormented and agonizing relationship.

Those who have been abused as small children often suffer from a conviction that awful things certainly happened, plus an inability to remember precisely what they were or to distinguish fact from fantasy. To write about these early experiences can seem essential, in order to objectify them, and yet doomed to frustration, because perhaps the truth can never be grasped. Petit's solution to this necessary obscurity is an extraordinary act of imagination. She uses the exotic imagery of the Amazon jungle, in both its animal and its human life, to convey the frightening, violent and 'far away' nature of the emotions and events described. It is this brilliant device that allows these poems to be truly created objects, and rescues them from being only 'confessional'. A remarkable poem called 'Self Portrait with Fire Ants' begins: 'To visit you, Father, I wear a mask of fire ants'. The ants attack her face as she speaks to him about his abandonment of her at the age of eight; they sting her eyes and swarm down her mouth into her stomach, and she imagines her father as an ant-eater, thrusting his tongue down her throat to catch them as once he French-kissed her baby brother. She ends: 'I can't remember what you did to me, but the ants know'.

Something unsayable is being conveyed here, a memory that is carried so to speak in the cells of the body, and any putting of it into direct words would be a shallow simplification, and perhaps untrue. The intolerable complexity of the emotions involved is also conveyed. This is by no means a simple picture of hatred for an abusing father – love, and longing, and sexual desire are also present – but again, to name them in this abstract form is to distort the reality Petit describes. She has working access, in such a poem, to the imaginative levels at which dreams are created.

Other poems, such as 'Trophy' and 'My Father's Body', in which with loving sado-masochism she goes into the technical detail of creating a shrunken head or a shrunken whole-body, take us yet further into excruciating realms. Not everyone will wish to accompany her there. Yet perhaps one of the functions of poetry is to be a bathysphere to penetrate into hidden abysses of feeling, and, as long as one can return to the surface, that deep contact can be integrating and energizing.

And sometimes, in spite of what I have said about memory, these poems convey what is surely the lived truth of childhood experience. 'The Magma Room' begins in a way that is utterly convincing:

> Then his window turned to quartz crystal
> and his curtains to rock.
> I was back in the magma chamber
> of my childhood.

After her father's death, Petit discovers he is not so easily parted from. She dreams of pouring his ashes into a fissure in the ocean bed, but he remains persistently present:

> Slap your tail fluke
> and I will follow in your wake.
> I who wanted a leviathan for a father
> will sink through the singing storeys of the sea.
> ('The Whale Father')

The beauty of the language tells its own story. This is not a rant against the father, Sylvia Plath-style; nor self-exculpation like Ted Hughes's *Birthday Letters*; we share in her colossal conflict between hatred and outrage, on the one hand, and love and longing, on the other. The poems that result are extraordinary, sometimes beautiful, sometimes terrifying.

A final short group of poems is entitled 'The Vineyard'. After the death of both her parents, Petit inherited this small property from her mother. She attempts in these poems to come to terms with her mother's thirty years of manic-depressive illness, to make through ordinary earth and moss and sun-warmed stone a contact with the woman her mother might have been – to 'mend' her mother's 'crooked' face and hold her secure in memory. She imagines sitting clasping her mother's shoulder 'so that neither of us knows / who is mother and who is daughter'. We find no easy resolution in this collection, but instead, lucid and courageous poems in which the daughter reaches to encompass experiences that neither parent could manage or take responsibility for. This work deserves enormous praise.

41 (Spring 2002)

Billy Collins, Looking Somewhat Keatsian

Kathryn Maris interviews the US Poet Laureate

There are moments in a conversation with US Poet Laureate Billy Collins when he sounds just like his poems. When fantasizing, for example, about the most useful criticism he could offer many of his workshop students, he deadpans in his low, drowsy reading voice: 'Stop writing. You are not cut out for this. Please, do something else'. His statements favour directness and clarity, as do his poems, which he describes as composed from a 'simple palette'. Perhaps by way of explanation, he says he often reads from an anthology of Chinese poems before sitting down to write his own work 'just because of its simplicity'.

Absent in his directness is any note of the pretentious or pedantic. This is again like his poems, which, he says, 'write against the posturing' of a certain kind of poetry that over-exalts itself or employs a grand, all-knowing tone. And finally: his poems are funny. And so is he. He lets it be known, however, that he is no glorified comedian. 'I just see humour as the correct view of the world,' he explains, 'because the world is so full of incongruities and imbalances and absurdities. So humour is not something I'm "putting on". Humour is the lens I'm looking through. It's a way of perceiving things – which is not the same as making a joke'.

It does seem, though, that Collins is often reduced to the label 'funny poet'. When American poet Jorie Graham introduced her first poem at the Coffee House reading series at the Troubadour in London, she warned, 'Tonight the gravedigger is in town. If you want "funny" you'll have to wait until next week when Billy Collins is here'. Nevertheless it's a label that seems to work in his favour, apparently explaining, at least in part, his popularity among readers on this side of the Atlantic who often say his poems appeal to the British aesthetic. When asked about this, he looks surprised and seems to negate the statement. 'Well, I wasn't aware that my poems did appeal to the British. I know this new book [*Nine Horses*] is selling well, but in fact when I read in England or Ireland, I notice that some of my poems sound very American. For example, I have a poem in which I mention a state flower, but to a British ear it could easily sound like "an estate flower"'. But he adds that in general he tries to avoid 'Americanisms' and hopes the simplicity of his syntax and diction makes his poems 'a little more universal' than they might otherwise be.

He is not surprised to hear that his relative fame in the UK is an anomaly, and that many American poets he would consider household names are not known at all here. He knows the reverse is true too, and acknowledges that the cross-cultural flow of British and American poetry is poor in general. In his view, English, Scottish and Welsh poetry tends to be obscured by Irish poetry in the US. He explains, 'Irish poetry has become quite popular in America and is widely read, probably because of Seamus Heaney who, by fulfilling a certain image of the Irish poet, partly accounts for the popularity of people like Paul Muldoon, Eavan Boland, Eamon Grennan and Paul Durcan, many of whom teach at American universities'. He also attributes the knowledge gap to publishing, saying 'A lot of British poets just aren't published in the States very widely. Whereas in the 1960s, Al Alvarez came out with an anthology called *The New Poetry*, which was published by Penguin and widely available in the States. That introduced people like Thom Gunn and Ted Hughes and lots of others to an American audience'.

He adds that 'Carol Ann Duffy is probably one of the most popular poets in England, but she's virtually unknown in America. And Simon Armitage is another. People who keep up with poetry would probably know of them. But the market in America is so flooded with poetry – there are so many books of poetry that come out every year – that it's enough to keep up with the American poetry scene let alone the British'. He says he intends to discuss the problem, Poet Laureate to Poet Laureate, with Andrew Motion, who, he laments, 'is another poet who's not really known in the US. He's known for his biography of Larkin, and by people who know who the poet laureate of Britain is, but it's hard to think of any English poet who is alive and widely read'.

But, of course, 'known' is a relative word, especially when talking about poetry. He attributes poetry's dwindling readership in the US to insufficient education early on in school, a conclusion drawn by many in this country too. Indeed, one of Collins's chief contributions as US Poet Laureate has been Poetry 180, a project which assigns each of the one hundred and eighty days in the American school year a poem – to be read in assemblies, in the classroom or simply to be posted on a bulletin board. The poems are contained on the Poetry 180 website – which gets one to two million hits a month – and also in an anthology by the same name, a book which he hopes will be published in the UK by Picador sometime in the future. Has Poetry 180 worked? 'Hundreds of schools are using it,' he says. 'Sometimes they don't read a poem every day; they might read a poem every Monday, for example.' He adds, 'High school teachers love it. They say it's a really good way of getting students interested in poetry. Because if you put out one hundred and eighty hooks, it would be a hopelessly dense student who fails to respond to all one hundred and eighty. It gets students over "poem phobia". And it rinses out the position, "I hate poetry. Poetry sucks"'. He chose every one of the poems, all of which can be described as contemporary and accessible, himself. He describes the process of sitting in Poets House, a vast poetry library in New York City, day after day, by saying, 'It took a long, long time. I had to read a lot of bad poems'.

On the subject of bad poetry, he disagrees with one of his predecessors in the position of US Poet Laureate, Robert Pinsky, who held the title in the late 1990s and used to assert that even bad poetry was good for poetry, for it raised awareness and gave people pleasure. But Collins refutes this unapologetically: 'Bad poetry is bad for poetry. The trouble with poetry is that it's too easy to write. It doesn't require any knowledge. You can't just pick up a cello and start playing. And you can't just get some oil paints and start painting with them, you have to know how to mix them. There's knowledge involved in playing the piano or making a piece of sculpture or dancing. But poetry just requires a piece of paper. And that's why there's so much bad stuff around'. He pauses and tries to remember a quote on this subject, but cannot

attribute it and only manages to paraphrase it: 'If you went to a piano concert and it became painfully and immediately clear in the first couple of minutes or seconds that the pianist didn't know how to play the piano, you would walk out, or you would ask for your money back. But we go to poetry readings and sit through excruciating boredom sometimes and just take it as a matter of course'.

Poetry readings are another bugbear for him. In an interview three years ago, he described them as a closed circuit: poets coming to hear other poets read, often with ulterior motives. Has his view on this changed? 'Well, this sounds immodest, but I think some of my readings are bringing in a broader audience who don't necessarily have a vested interest in writing poetry, but I still think generally there is that "closed circuit" aspect. And this is especially evident in open mic readings. Basically what these open mic readers are doing there is waiting to get up and read themselves, not actually listening to the featured poets. Or they're there to make connections, to hand the poet a manuscript, for example'. If this sounds like biting the hand that feeds him, it is not the only time he does so; he is equally disillusioned with writing workshops, though teaching them at Lehman College in the Bronx, New York City, is how he makes part of his living. (He also teaches literature at Lehman, which he enjoys more. 'I prefer subject matter to student poetry.') He views writing as a solo activity, and finds the collaborative aspect of a workshop unnatural. He himself never attended a workshop, and claims never to have had any mentors.

When asked if he sees any value at all in creative writing degrees, he says, 'Yes. They create a wider, smarter readership of poetry'. But don't they falsely encourage students to believe that they, too, will become well known as poets, or have teaching jobs? Collins shrugs. 'It's the same kind of argument as teaching kids in inner cities basketball and letting them dream of being an NBA basketball star.' Such comments suggest Collins to be a hardboiled New Yorker of some other era, an image that seems further supported by the tough-guy drink he orders: 'Jameson, straight up'. Born in Manhattan in 1941, he is in fact a lifelong New Yorker. His father was what the English might call an upwardly mobile working-class man, who later started a middle-class business and moved his family out to the wealthier suburbs. Perplexed by Collins's ambition to pursue a PhD in literature and teach, his father saw it as a step down. (He didn't live to see Collins become Poet Laureate.) Collins says, 'When I think of my father's reaction to my chosen profession, I think of that quote by Thomas Jefferson, which goes something like, "My father was a farmer so that I could be a lawyer, so that my son could be a poet"'. He says he met with other forms of discouragement on his road to becoming a poet, including a priest at his Catholic college who dismissed his poems in the college literary magazine with, 'Anything you write before the age of twenty-six doesn't count'. He also remembers being interviewed by the college president for a radio show at around the same time. The college president told Collins, 'Of course you'll never win the Pulitzer prize with these poems', and continued on as though his judgement were self-evident. Collins explains, 'Now, I haven't won the Pulitzer Prize and I probably never will, but I felt like saying, "I'll show you, you bastard!"'. He says these were positive turning points in his life because 'it's good to be discouraged. I've responded better to discouragement than to pats on the back. Because they're challenges'.

One challenge he has not risen to is the novel, a genre that sometimes tempts poets out of poetry for a while. On this, he says, 'You have to be interested in other people to be a novelist. But to be a poet you just have to be obsessively interested in yourself, looking out your own window at the world'. Is that why so many of his poems contain the image of the window, and the speaker looking out of it? 'Yes, it's sort of an epistemological position – standing in an interior and looking out at the world. Which I then try to make fun of in the poem'.

Does he feel, as a poet, that he is eternally outside the action, looking in? 'Yeah. That's probably right. It's probably an image that comes from the idea of the gazer. It's a figure lifted from British Romanticism. That is to say a fellow who falls asleep in a field, who watches clouds and daydreams – a kind of Keatsian languorous figure.' By the end of the interview, he looks more Keatsian than he might realize. He has done readings and interviews all week, and his interview with me is sandwiched between two others in the same day. As I pack up and get ready to say goodbye, we make small talk about his hotel, The Gore. I tell him that I have bad associations with it: my father-in-law fainted there a year ago on a hot summer's evening. He responds with a classically Billy Collins quip: 'Was he giving interviews all day?'

46 (Autumn 2003)

To Flutter the Soul

Editorial by *Maurice Riordan*

Ford Madox Ford, who edited the *English Review* early in the last century, tells how late one evening he was reading submissions and briskly dropping most of them – the melancholy routine of all editors – in the reject pile. He picked up a short story by someone he'd never heard of, read a few sentences, and popped it among the acceptances. His secretary – it was a different era – asked him if he'd discovered another genius. 'It's a big one this time,' he told her. The story was 'Odour of Chrysanthemums' by D.H. Lawrence, which had been copied and put in the post by Jessie Chambers. It was Lawrence's first publication.

I have been reminded of Ford's anecdote often this past summer, as I've sifted through my own pile of submissions. Is there a genius to be discovered in here? And then the worrying thought: what if there is and I should miss him or her? What made Ford so sure? Well, he gives a helpful analysis of what he quickly recognized in Lawrence: the particularity, the intimacy, the visualness of the writing – each of them qualities the novice writer should aim for.

They are, too, qualities the attentive reader can recognize and linger over. But, alas, it's the instantaneous decision an editor needs. The subconscious response preceding active interest is what may save him from the ignominy of not seeing the hidden genius. Luckily poems have, I believe far more so than prose, an impact which is immediate and preanalytic. Emily Dickinson has often described this in physical terms – notoriously as having the top of her head blown off! Robert Graves had a more homely, if effectively gender-specific, test for a true poem. He found when he recited the lines they caused the hairs to bristle on his chin. Doing so before the mirror helped him with his morning shave.

Unfortunately, I don't have the facial growth to put Graves's test into practice on an editorial basis, but I do tend to work through my pile in a sleepy unshaven early morning state of mind.

I'm needing to be woken up! And indeed just about every poem I set aside has administered something like a mild electric shock, a tingling of the nerve ends even as I'm no more than a line or two into reading it. On occasion in fact I feel a charge from a poem before I start reading. This isn't as loopy as it sounds. I'd suggest it is an effect of *claritas*, the 'radiance' a poem has because of its formal completeness. Sometimes the very look of a poem on the page causes it to jump towards one, as the moon does when it emerges from behind thin cloud.

Sometimes, that is – since a poem's formal quality is not necessarily visual. This is more true nowadays because poetry relies on the manner of prose. A conversational pitch, clarity of detail and the coherence of the sentence are virtues it often shares with decent fiction. Yet this is actually a guise, an apparent and superficial resemblance. At heart, a poem will have what the Italian Romantic poet Leopardi called 'rapidity and concision of style' lifting it on to a higher plane. Rapidity is the interesting one here and Leopardi elaborates on what he means by it in conspicuously physical terms. A poem, he continues, should 'keep the mind in constant and lively movement and action, transporting it suddenly, and often abruptly, from one thought, image, idea, or obiect to another, and often to one very remote and different; so that the mind must work hard to overtake them all, and, as it is flung about here and there, feels invigorated, as one does in walking quickly or in being carried along by swift horses'.

That's the sort of stuff I need in the morning to get the adrenaline working. I sense almost immediately, or rather I *hear*, an athleticism in a poem, a tightness

of line and a syntactical speed and co-ordination that distinguish it utterly from the norms of prose. There are of course other qualities a poem must have if it is to draw one back, if it is to excite many minds, if it is to prove memorable. But I believe it is the sudden feeling of acceleration in one's attention that first announces the presence of a true poem, and first causes it, in Leopardi's phrase, to 'flutter the soul'.

52 (Autumn 2005)

A Poet You May Want To Know Better: Eugenio Montale

Jamie McKendrick profiles a Nobel Laureate whose stature is a monument that fills the whole piazza

Over the last fifty years, no other Italian poet except Dante has been so often translated into English as Montale. Googling Amazon for book publications confirms this guess. And that's not to speak of the innumerable one-off versions by contemporary poets, nor of the burgeoning critical industry in English, let alone the mountainous one in Italy. This kind of fame has the effect of flattening out the context his poems emerge from as well as crowding out the reputations of several remarkable contemporaries and successors. It's a monument that fills the whole piazza.

Writing about Edgar Allan Poe, Montale asked: 'Has he been favoured by his myth, the legend made of him? We have no difficulty in believing that, but the destiny of poets is also a part of their work'. Criticism should have some 'difficulty' with this belief, and should surely try to disentangle the work from its reception. Montale's reputation is distinct from Poe's in that his eminence abroad corresponds to his fame in Italy, even if, there, it isn't bestowed nearly so exclusively. The Nobel Prize can only have helped, though Salvatore Quasimodo, an earlier winner, hasn't taken, over here, (or taken over, here,) to anything like the same extent. In Montale's case there may also be some kind of a return of favours: Italian critics often remark, sometimes rather vaguely, on the ascendancy of Anglo-American influences on his work, from Hopkins and Dickinson to Eliot. These claims are unconvincing, but there is a kind of muted irony, a use of barbed understatement, in his writing that might specially recommend him to an Anglo-Saxon readership. The fact that it comes accompanied by sun-baked Ligurian coastal views, by a sense of nature in midday, dog-day extremis – especially in his first and most translated work, *Ossi di seppia* (Cuttlefish Bones) – only serves both to exoticize and to authenticate the mode.

Ossi di seppia, first published in 1925 when the poet was twenty-nine, must be one of the most astonishing debut poetry volumes of the last century. The earliest poem included, written when he was twenty, 'Meriggiare pallido e assorto', is a hymn to stunned inertia:

> To shelter at noon, pallid and rapt,
> back against a scalding orchard wall;
> to hear from in the thick of briars
> blackbirds' blatter, the slither of adders.
>
> To spy how over the tares' stalks, along cracks
> in the earth, lines of red ants that break
> and close ranks, intertwine
> atop miniature haystacks.
> To observe through boughs the sea's
> distant shimmering of scales
> while from bald heights the cicadas
> unleash their tremulous calls.
>
> Then walking out in the dazzling sun,
> to feel, grimly amazed, how all
> of life and its drudgery is in
> this act of following a wall
> whose top is harled with jagged glass.

This translation of mine falls some way short of the complex acoustics of the original. Although Montale's poems will tend towards subtler and more oblique effects, the very stated moral in the original poem's last stanza is offset and faceted by an ingenious series of interlocking rhymes (abbaglio / meraviglia / travaglio / muraglia / bottiglia). The poem's structure is basic: static infinitives organize

each of the four stanzas – meriggiare, ascoltare (stanza 1), spiar (2), osservare (3), sentire (4). But the senses they call on – especially that of hearing – are vividly alert to a bristling panorama of small-scale activity. The 'k' 'g' 'ch' and 'sh' sounds (schiocchi, frusci, veccia, s'intrecciano, formiche, biche, scaglie, cicale, calvi, picchi) are superbly orchestrated in the final line 'che ha in cima cocci aguzzi di bottiglia'. (It's worth remembering that in Italian the double consonants are sounded.) Though the form looks at first conventional, there are irregular lines, and even the rhyming has odd qualities such as the already noted final stanza and the hypermetric rhyme 'veccia / s'intrecciano'. The harsh consonantal quality of the writing and rhyming is reminiscent of Dante's 'rime petrose' (stony rhymes), which particularly in this section of the book (the actual 'Ossi brevi') might be termed 'bony rhymes'.

This early poem also introduces the idea of the wall, a limit to perceptions, which will, in a number of transformations, be a signal motif throughout his work. It appears in this volume's poem 'In limine' as the 'erto muro' (sheer wall), as well as 'the net', a break in which will allow the addressee to escape. Elsewhere this image becomes a veil, a seal, a husk, and most famously 'un'aria di vetro' (literally, an air of glass), a glass screen. Though some of the poems are addressed to absent people, the poems are essentially self-communing, or rather enact an engagement of the self with the natural world, minutely and brilliantly apprehended, but always acknowledging some prohibiting veto, some wall that blocks human access to the primary and Edenic. Frequent bird, animal and plant imagery is constantly set against the defining backdrop of the sea. The risk of solipsism is not always averted, but the rewards of the poems are in their chaffing, percussive musicality, the precision of the imagery and the vast reach of language that blends the colloquial, even occasionally dialect words, with the offbeat and recondite (here, for example, the verb 'meriggiare' is uncommon and literary).

The negative constructions that abound in his work are already fully present in this first book (most famously in those lines from another *Osso*, 'Don't ask us for the word…': 'all we can tell you today is /

what we don't want, what we aren't') and announce a sceptical, resistant sensibility. Montale is a poet of resonant negatives, an anti-rhetorical stance probably taken with D'Annunzio in his sights. This cast of mind will equip him well for the years of Fascism, and *Le occassioni* (The Occasions), his second and perhaps greatest book, takes what was essentially a contract with the natural world and exposes it to the social world, to the terrafirma of culture, as he was to call it.

Le occasioni was published in 1939, its composition more or less coinciding with the poet's residence in Florence. The move towards greater obliquity, or Hermeticism, can be seen in the sequence 'Mottetti', where single images, or 'flashes' (the English word is used by Montale), suddenly illuminate a whole psychological complex, and then, just as abruptly, vanish. The poems are more fractured, sometimes even febrile in their imagery. For all that the personal experience these poems record seems under increasing external threat, the writing itself has an unwavering assurance. Pasolini characterized Montale's poetry as the product of a wounded, bourgeois sensibility, but this unnecessarily limits the scope of the poems. The critic Glauco Cambon notes that though the First World War, in which Montale was a combatant, rarely surfaces in his poems, 'the repercussion of that first holocaust of the century is to be felt in the atmosphere of hopelessness which recurrently visits his poetry', and his refusal of any further ideological conscription is informed by that experience.

Another feature that emerges fully in these poems is the presence of a 'tu', often a woman, whom the poem addresses. As with the dedicatory poem of *Ossi di seppia*, these figures (who will come to be known as Clizia, Arletta, etc.) are often the repositories of the poet's fugitive hopes for an alternative to the increasingly sinister world the poems register. Those years of, and leading up to, the Second World War might not seem the most auspicious of times for a poet to try to re-animate a Provençal or 'stilnovistic' convention, in which a departing or absent female figure becomes a crucial – both spiritual and erotic – governing principle of the poem. But this renewal of a tradition is what Montale undertakes. And, by anchoring this principle within the menace and finely observed phenomena of the times, in 'Dora Markus', 'News from Mount Amiata' and 'The Coastguard's House', for example, he achieves effects of extraordinary intensity.

For those wanting to learn more about this topic, and much else about the individual poems of the first three volumes, Jonathan Galassi's notes to his translation (Montale, *Collected Poems 1920–1954*) offer an incisive summary of a range of critical material on the poet. When I reviewed the book, I objected to this long coda of footnotes the poems had to drag behind them, but have since been grateful for their existence. Still, the question remains as to how fruitful all the endless research into the symbolic properties of these addressees really is, and it's a question about which Montale himself remains playfully sceptical. These absent presences, though they may involve actual figures such as Irma Brandeis, a Jewish friend and Italianist who returned to the US in 1938, are also poignant residues of the poet himself, the 'signs' of life of a spirit that hasn't been deadened by the times it lives in. The 'tu' which, Montale himself joked in a later poem, has become a critical institution, is also something that belongs within the consciousness of the poem, a fugitive other. And so much of the finest of Montale's writing is pitched towards these curtailed impressions or flashes that vouchsafe a sense, however menaced, of a better life.

In *La bufera* (1956), the third volume, which completes his major work, a woman addressee (probably Clizia) gloriously re-emerges in one of his greatest poems, 'L'anguilla' ('The Eel'). Another, more earthbound, figure, 'La Volpe' (the Vixen) – identified as the poet Maria Luisa Spaziani – provides a contrast to the ethereal and transcendental Clizia. Oddly, Robert Lowell's translation of 'The Eel' incorporates the next, untitled poem, which is addressed to 'La Volpe' ('Se t' hanno assomigliato...') as part of 'The Eel'. I suspect this was done inadvertently through his use of George R. Kay's *Penguin Book of Italian Verse* as the source. There, the second poem follows 'The Eel' without title, so that a reader not paying attention to the conventions of the book (first word in caps; first letter in larger size for each new poem) might easily assume the two separate poems were two stanzas of the same poem. Had Lowell referred to an Italian text – or even looked more closely at Kay – the error wouldn't have occurred. Apart from links in the imagery, the two poems in the Italian have interesting formal similarities, each being thirty lines long without a full-stop and ending in a question. Though the two poems seem to be addressed to different women, the deliberate formal connections between them may have added to Lowell's conviction that the two belonged together, and may even account for the way Lowell has badly misconstrued the final question of 'L'anguilla'. (His book, *Imitations*, prints both Italian 'titles', separated by a semi-colon, after his translation, which would suggest that by the time of printing, Lowell had been made aware of his initial mistake – but, by that stage, I suspect he was committed to the version as it stands.) Given the licence he claims for his versions, why shouldn't he call them (make them) 'sisters', to reprise Montale's question at the end of 'The Eel'? I think the answer is that they aren't, and Lowell, for all the energy of his version, leaves 'The Eel' in a sorry tangle.

Several subsequent volumes followed in a far quicker succession that wasn't to be interrupted by his death in 1981. Beginning with *Satura* (1971) – effectively considered the cut-off point – these works have a drier, more casual tone. Their manner of de-mythologizing the earlier work has caused some dismay in critics such as the poet Giovanni Raboni, as if they were not just a falling off but a betrayal. Montale himself acknowledges that the three first books constitute a complete entity, calling them his three canticles. Many of these later poems have the air of aftermath, of having outlived their occasions; and yet though they lack the pitch of intensity and the musicality of the earlier work, they can still call on his style of 'condensed despatch'. In contrast to the shadowy, supramundane, female figures that populate his earlier poems, the elegies for his wife, Drusilla Tanzi, nicknamed La Mosca, in *Satura*'s 'Xenia' sequences, tenderly and ironically record a vivid, actual presence. Even the briefest of these work well within the sequence: 'Listening was the only way you had of seeing. / Now the telephone bill's a damn sight cheaper'. (His wife's short-sightedness is a recurrent image.)

A poem like 'In the Window' could represent this late manner:

Birds that bode ill – say owls of one type
or another – only turn up live
in undernourished Kasbahs or else stuffed
in the glass cases of misanthropes. And if
a swallow should happen to build its nest
in a vent or flue and an incautious tenant
snuffed it from the fumes: that would be a one-off
and not enough to change the total picture.

Considering the abundance, one could say excess, of translations of his best known work, mightn't these canny and durable late poems – relatively ignored in the English-speaking world – deserve more attention?

52 (Autumn 2005)

Losers Weepers

Editorial by *Martha Kapos*

In *Finders Keepers*, Seamus Heaney gives a poignant account of the anxiety he experienced when he first encountered the poetry of T.S. Eliot. This was at a time, in the 1950s, when Eliot was the light and the way: a name synonymous with modern poetry itself. A volume of the collected poems was posted to Heaney at school 'like a food parcel', yet instead of supplying a longed-for pleasure, the words produced in him something resembling a panic attack. They were on a wavelength as inaudible to him as if they had been the squeaks of a bat. Physical symptoms – a growing lump in the throat, a tightening of the diaphragm – were not relieved by subsequent readings. Instead, and for years, 'Eliot scared me off, made me feel humiliated and small, made me want to call on the Mother of Readers to come quick, to make sense of it, to give me the secure pacifier of a para-phrasable meaning.'

Was he exaggerating? I don't think so. At the same time as inviting us to identify with the plight of the schoolboy, Heaney also says that the acute anxiety he describes is not a schoolboy reaction, or not merely. We are all learning from Eliot, and others, that a poem can never take us entirely beyond its language to a brightly lit and focused place – as if 'obscurity' were murky water that intelligent reading could render transparent and clear. 'A poem must resist the intelligence almost successfully' (Stevens) is the downright sort of assertion it's easy enough to accept. But what is so attractive in Heaney is the frankness with which he admits to the anxiety of not understanding.

When Stevens writes 'A man and a woman / Are one' we can understand without difficulty, but 'A man and a woman and a blackbird / Are one' and we are flummoxed. We set off on a path in the anxious hope that we will arrive sooner or later at a single main sense for the poem that will include the blackbird. But, perhaps, losing our bearings is a fundamental part of the process. The playground game of Heaney's title 'Finders Keepers' has loss as its counterpart.

A statement Heaney makes in a later chapter revises my image of the path: 'Poetry is more a threshold than a path – one constantly approached and constantly departed from at which reader and writer undergo in their different ways the experience of being at the same time summoned and released'. Perhaps it was the spatial imagery of the threshold as well as the theme of anxiety and loss that made me want to look again at the story about his grandson I'd read years ago in Freud's 'Beyond the Pleasure Principle'.

The little boy, in an attempt to cope with his mother's alarming ability to vanish from his sight for hours at a time, plays a repeated game. Holding one end of a string attached to a cotton reel he hurls it over the edge of his cot and then spools it in, accompanying its arrival and departure with the words 'Here' and 'Gone'. This stark game enacts his mother's presence and absence – or so psychoanalysts say.

Part of the appeal of Freud's story about his grandson, seen as the figure of the poet, is the idea that the desire for presence and the effect of absence are implicated in each other and even animate each

other permanently. The game of Here and Gone is one that the poet plays in the little theatre of each sentence. With the Mother of Readers holding the poet's hand, words play their familiar roles with a reassuring and consoling logic. Here is the static noun, the active verb, the spaces and perspectives of the prepositions. And above all, here is the rigid duality and separateness of subjects and objects. In fact, the necessary grammar of the sentence itself slots the world into arrangements on which our day-to-day sanity depends. This, as Yeats might say, is the language of the breakfast table.

But suddenly, within the reassuring flow of sentences, disturbances are created. Words are arranged into lines, lines into rows. They are turned over, turned towards each other to make musical patterns – to mention only a few of the huge disruptions poetic form introduces into language. Metaphor takes away literal meaning and Mother has fallen through a trapdoor out of sight. We are left in the scary yet vivid zone Yeats described as 'phantasmagoria', where our awareness of the subjectivity of objects and the objectivity of subjective emotion becomes uniquely possible. It is here that we begin to discern the reshaped and recreated meanings of poetry.

57 (Summer 2007)

Lost on the Moon

Peter Porter brings home to earth the work of *John Ashbery*

Towards the end of that sprawling humanist cavalcade, Ariosto's *Orlando Furioso*, one of the more significant dramatis personae, Astolfo, a sanguinary paladin, is carried off to the moon by an enchantment (which in Ariosto usually means some neurasthenic madness derived from love). His chief discovery there is that the surface of the moon abounds in objects which people on earth have lost. There is a sub-Christian notion in this – not too long before Ariosto, and near his home town of Ferrara, Italy's second great modern saint, Anthony of Padua, lived out his ministry. To this day the pious and the hopeful pray to Anthony to find them things they've lost. In Ariosto, it is, of course, not so much chairs and tables or bequests which they have been deprived of as emotions: love, friendship, reciprocal admiration etc. But Ariosto, ever the dry and practical poet, emphasizes that the moon is a repository, junkyard even, of humanity's misplaced possessions. The problem is how to get these things back to the earth, where we can rejoice once more in their possession.

I find John Ashbery's poetry can be, if not fully understood, then at least appreciated if I think of it as made of verbal structures derived from everyday life on earth but magically manoeuvred to a newly created life on the moon. One of Ashbery's most acute critics, Stephen Burt, in a recent *TLS* article, emphasizes that no contemporary poet deals more unflinchingly with existence as we know it in the busy huddle of urban living. More even than Auden, Ashbery is unafraid of common figures of speech, proverbial utterances and even the stalest clichés of daily communication. A reader need not know what got into the newspapers during the life of Wallace Stevens to feel at ease reading his verse. Ashbery, however, is with us at the check-out, on holiday, watching TV, dousing ourselves in Hollywood fragrances, listening to our doctors and even thinking about the way modern man dies. He also knows British and wider European Literature, and dovetails it in an unforced way into his poetry. He is not a spurner of any kind of elitism; he just knows that words are kinned outside their specialisms and genres. His titles are not as highbrowly teasing as Stevens's, but they tweak the broadcast pieties of academic English. Daffy Duck can go to Hollywood but so can Andrew Marvell's Tom May be put drunk into the Packet Boat. Though Ashbery is a difficult poet, claimed by his followers as the true inheritor of Modernism, I am convinced that his poetry, highly recognizable in its lineaments, is something more original than run-of-the-mill American experiment – namely Moon Poetry. We find the things we love in it, but we cannot always recognize where they come from, or what they are doing, or bring them home to earth to live with us.

Another metaphor for the Ashbery method, or more properly the Ashbery ambience, comes from conjuring up the extraordinary, detailed tapestries of the late medieval period, such as those in the Musée de Cluny. In the 'Lady and the Unicorn' series, the background is often what is known as 'milles fleures', an amazing carpet of individual blooms related to each other but serving a greater purpose, a sort of Field of the Cloth of Life. With Ashbery it is the case of 'milles contes'; dozens of stories, mostly cut off in the telling, are gathered together in any one poem, in defiance of plot and objective reason. Such writing amounts to a pleasing bewilderment of dramas, an untheological pandemonium, as anecdotes converse with one another, relying on the poet's verbal skills to keep the traffic flowing. One result of this has been his much remarked reliance on non sequitur. While his more intransigent admirers think this is a good thing, others of us believe it doesn't work quite like that.

His best poems can be gems with many faces, yet are always of consistent substance. 'These Lacustrine Cities', 'Grand Galop', 'Saying It to Keep It from Happening', 'And *Ut Pictura Poesis* is Her Name', 'Syringa' and the stateliest of his long poems, 'Self-Portrait in a Convex Mirror', are all flashing different lights at the same time. When this happens within a dramatic monologue, a kind of radiant if sometimes protracted Browningesque conviction unfolds. Often his sense of Victorian responsibility – allied to a fondness for detail derived from Victorian Literature (chiefly English, not American) – makes his poems much easier for the reader to enter than those of many of his contemporaries. It is many years since a major poet's tone has been more important than his moral concerns or his aesthetic. Ultimately, we don't need interpreters while on his moonscape. We have a pentecostal willingness to understand, or at least to be entertained.

But such prodigality can become insufferable at very great length. You might be able to dredge fascinating local insights at any moment from such extended poems as the antiphonal 'Litany', 'A Wave', 'The System', 'And the Stars Were Shining' or book-length works such as the almost interminable *Flow Chart* and that teasing burlesque, *Girls on the Run*; but more frequently you will be deafened by the noise of the poems' sound-floor. Success with the public and the critics has encouraged Ashbery not only to write at greater length but to prefer a garrulous free association to more poetic songlines and to print the result frequently as prose. For such an instinctive formalist, he has shown little interest in developing strict stanza-shapes and divisions; his quatrains have ragged lines and seldom rhyme. In this he departs from the example of Wallace Stevens and Auden, his two father figures if not necessarily models. Stevens rhymes only intermittently, but is much more regular in metre, happy to indulge in pavanes and threnodies. While Ashbery has been fond of pantoums, sonnets of various sorts, and occasionally of villanelles and sestinas, his preferred way of dealing with the richness of the past is to dissolve our poetic inheritance into an essence, so the reader feels the gamey disquiet of Beddoes or even *The Golden Treasury* as a ghostly presence in poems of a deliberately dandified novelty. There is one constant. We are in the self-governing realm of language. Words rule; form follows.

While writing this short and impertinent assessment, I have returned to (or sometimes encountered for the first time) almost all of Ashbery's copious poetic output. As music critics like to assert, there is a recognizable line running through his oeuvre. Late Ashbery is more deliquescent than his early and formative work – it sometimes amounts to violent electrical interference to poems you imagine were more straightforward imagined *ab ovo*. But there is never a complete loss of direction or abandonment of a binding force field. Reading his most recent collection, *A Worldly Country*, for last year's T.S. Eliot prize, I was struck by a couple of instances of poems which could well have been included in *Some Trees* or *The Tennis Court Oath*.

The finest of Ashbery's achievements to my taste remain in three middle-period volumes – *Self-Portrait in A Convex Mirror*, *Houseboat Days* and *Shadow Train*. The title poem of the first of these is as commanding and transfiguring in its way as Stevens's 'Aesthetique Du Mal' or 'Notes Towards a Supreme Fiction', but with an additional and unexpected authority gained by lacking Stevens's omnipresent smoothness. It's almost like early Pisan sculpture in its roughness – Nicola and Giovanni Pisano versus Jacopo della Quercia and Donatello. Ashbery here becomes the heir to such extended analyses of human endeavour and artistic wilfulness as Browning's 'Bishop Blougram's Apology' and 'Mr. Sludge the Medium'. Taking Parmiagianino's self-distortion in his mirror as starting-point, Ashbery moves into the hinterland of identity, and finds both the inwardness of speculation and the outwardness of the soul's passage through existence. He points out that Latin for mirror is 'speculum' – at any moment you may find that what you see is not what you have been seeing or what you have anticipated would be shown. My sense of Pisan roughness comes from the poem's eschewing any lyrical surface – the lyricism stays in the notions and in the ever-spreading associations. It is a curiously old-fashioned way of composing poetry: you put more in; you extend and develop; you remain conjecturing to the end. The whole lengthy discourse is a kind of 'exploded' philosophy. It may be the best way to embody Whitman's self-congratulatory admission that he contradicted himself:

The momentum of a conviction that had been
    building
Mere forgetfulness cannot remove it
Nor wishing bring it back, as long as it remains
The white precipitate of its dream
In the climate of sighs flung across our world,
A cloth over a birdcage.

In a later poem Ashbery asks 'Who knows how much there can be / of any one thing if another stops existing?' His answer to such a question is usually 'probably nothing'. As Stephen Burt writes, 'no poet has written our inevitable deaths into such daily, here-and-now poetry, or done so with so equable a demeanour'. Ashbery's Orpheus poem 'Syringa' ends with an acceptance of death's democratic principles – let the great artists protest as they may.

Stellification
Is for the few, and comes about much later
When all record of these people and their lives
have disappeared into libraries, onto microfilm.

A few are still interested in them. 'But what about
So-and-so?' is still asked on occasion. But they lie
Frozen and out of touch until an arbitrary chorus
Speaks of a totally different incident with a similar
    name
In whose tale are hidden syllables
Of what happened so long before that
In some small town, one indifferent summer.

I find this level-headed reticence more reassuring
than Rilke's acrobatic transcendence. Perhaps it's a
good thing to live longer.

Despite the remarkable consistency of style
running through all Ashbery's work, there is a
perceptible difference of tone in his shorter poems,
especially when he groups them in sequences, as he
often does. His fondness for aphorisms worked
together, plus a winning terseness of effect, makes
the sequence in *Shadow Train* very attractive. Its
bizarria reinforces the unswervability of human fate,
but does so with a light touch. In 'Qualm' Ashbery
writes 'The agony is permanent / Rather than
eternal'. This is worthy of Lichtenberg and derives,
as his aphorisms do, from what another poet called
'real, visible, material, happiness'. Sometimes it
seems a discounting of the elaborate flourishes else-
where in Ashbery's poetry. By now, we, his readers,
should have discovered that we do not have to be
always on the moon to appreciate what he is telling
us.

61 (Autumn 2008)

Strange Fruit

Luke Kennard celebrates an underrated master

Francis Ponge was born in Montpellier in 1899. He
worked as a journalist during the First World War,
and was a book distributor for Hachette before being
drafted in 1938. His first and most famous collection,
Le Parti pris des choses (here translated as *The
Defence of Things*), was published in 1942, but had
been largely composed over the previous decades. He
rose to prominence in the late Fifties after his work

was celebrated in essays by Sartre and Camus (the
latter of whom he fought alongside in the Resist-
ance). Ponge is now better known in America than
Britain, perhaps an indication of our parochialism
(given that we could be standing at his graveside after
a relatively short train ride).

As we learn in Beverley Bie Brahic's introduction
to *Unfinished Ode to Mud*, a new English edition of
his prose poems, Ponge began, at the age of fourteen,
to read Émile Littré's extraordinary four-volume
dictionary of the French language, published in the
mid-nineteenth century, a work remarkable for its
detail and etymological scope. This early obsession
clearly formed Ponge's poetic style. His works
always concern (and take their titles from) a single
object – an orange, a door, a washpot or an electric
fire – which the poet proceeds to define. Com-
menting on his own poetics, Ponge attests, 'The
simplest way is to take up everything again from the
beginning, lie down on the grass, and start over, as if
one knew nothing'.

Ponge's definitions appeal to the senses in a
manner at once lyrical and strange. In 'Moss', we read
how 'A thousand little silk velvet rods crossed their
legs and sat down'. The candle is 'a singular plant
whose gleam turns furnished rooms to clumps of
shadow'. It eventually 'bends over its dish and
drowns in its food'. Ponge's work is to the dictionary
as gin is to water, which is to say not nearly so useful,
but much lovelier at the end of a tough day.

He can write with a sure-footed clarity that never-
theless makes us gleefully re-experience the simplest
act or thing:

Kings don't touch doors.

They do not know this bliss: to push one of those
large familiar panels gently or brusquely ahead of
oneself, to turn and put it back in its place – to hold
a door in one's arms. ...The bliss of getting a grip
on one of a room's tall obstacles by its belly's
porcelain knob...

('The Delights of the Door')

Defamiliarization, *der Verfremdungseffekt*, Mar-
tianism, call it what you will, in heavier hands can

come off as disastrously *faux-naif*, spurring the earthier reader, perhaps, to flip to the index to see how the poet defines a spade. The less tedious among us are free to enjoy 'Mistletoe' as 'fog-belt mimosa... Shipwrecks snagged to the branches of trees, at the low water level of December fogs'. Never have I resented my lethal feather-allergy more than when reading Ponge's contemplation of 'The Eiderdown' – which I'm not going to reprint here because I want you to buy this book and not just make do with the digest. He's a writer who makes you feel like writing – and that's really about as noble an end to writing as there can be.

Ponge's prose poems operate on two levels; he begins with a straightforward but nonetheless lyrical description of the object in question which then becomes inundated with double-meanings and derivations. The poem finishes with a coda that returns us to the object – from which we have usually travelled quite a distance. The description itself is remarkable in 'The Orange':

> As with the sponge, there is with the orange an aspiration to recover countenance after submitting to the test of expression. But where the sponge is unfailingly successful, the orange never is: its cells have burst, its tissues ripped.

The characterization applies not so much to the object as to its characteristics, which in this case aspire, submit and fail. In the second paragraph, this subtle personification is realized politically rather than whimsically:

> Must one take sides concerning these different ways of not withstanding oppression? – The sponge is just a muscle and fills up with air, with clean or dirty water, it all depends: a disgraceful performance. The orange has better taste, but it is too passive – and this fragrant sacrifice... really it submits too readily to its oppressor.

This description takes on a certain poignancy when Ponge's experience of withstanding Nazi oppression is taken into account. He joined the Resistance in the same year *Le Parti pris des choses* was published; a time when many writers and artists were keeping their heads down and getting on with their lives in a somewhat sponge-like fashion.

As with the imaginative leaps in Robert Bly's 'Deep Image' prose poems, the conceptual and the ethical are explored through the thing itself. If you like, in Ponge's work we start at the other side of metaphor, with the object facilitating the concept rather than the concept likened to the object. And this never feels forced, never feels any less than, well, *true*. A seemingly innocuous pebble takes on a curious resonance when we consider 'that because man doesn't generally put it to any practical use, it is stone still in its wild state, or at least undomesticated'.

Claimed by many factions and aesthetic movements throughout his career (surrealism, phenomenology, existentialism), Ponge finally aligned himself with none. It is its modest humanity and subtle deflation of the claims of Romanticism that continues to refresh and delight in the poetry today. As Patrick Meadows attests, 'It is to *things* that Ponge wanted to give a voice, thereby rejecting the notion of the divinely or supernaturally inspired poet in order to focus on the pleasurable description-definition of the neglected phenomena of material existence' (*Francis Ponge and the Nature of Things*, 1997). This, let's be honest, is something a reader might reasonably be interested in. On the other hand, the idea of the supernaturally inspired poet could only be of interest to similarly afflicted poets, whether out of sympathy or mutual justification. It is what Margaret Guiton calls 'that *ethics* as well as *poetics* of self-knowledge, irony, reasonableness and restraint' (*Francis Ponge: Selected Poems*, 1994). None of those things are typically associated with movements and factions; all of them are uncelebrated attributes of the prose poem, of which Ponge's work is exemplary. 'Unfinished Ode to Mud' begins: 'Mud pleases the noble of heart because it is constantly scorned'. It concludes: 'It tempts us to form, then in the end discourages us. So be it! And I cannot do better, to its glory, to its shame, than to write an ode diligently unfinished'.

Unfinished Ode to Mud is the first parallel text edition of Ponge's work I have come across. The numerous American editions I've enjoyed and consulted in the past have presented the translations only. This is an act of generosity as well as bravery; a tacit argument that poetry might be best translated and enjoyed in its original language side by side. At times the work complements the model of symbolism espoused by Mallarmé in the 1890s; it is the art of describing an object 'little by little so as to evoke a mood' through 'a series of decipherings'. This may be a misleading verb; such decoding will not necessarily lead us to a clearer truth about the object in question. In fact it's more likely to lead us deeper into the idiosyncrasies of the poet. The trick is to treat an object as if it *were* a code, as if all things were clues in some divine and impossible-to-grasp order that it is our job to guess at. This may not be the case, but hell, it's more fun than dancing. 'The Blackberries' begins:

On the typographic bushes of the poem, down a road leading neither out of things nor to the mind, certain fruits are formed of an agglomeration of spheres plumped with a drop of ink.

*

Black, pink, khaki together on the [cluster], they are more like the sight of a [haughty] family at its different ages than a strong temptation to picking.

In this passage we see a clear demarcation between first- and second-order imagery. Ponge's metaphor, above the star, has a literal, tangible property which allows him to swoop off tangentially beneath it. There is nothing visual about the correlation between the multicoloured blackberry and the haughty family; yet the reader is already on Ponge's side thanks to the sensory accuracy of the 'drop of ink', and we feel we must recoil from the spoiled blackberry in just the same way we would recoil from the spoiled children and pompous elders. What is more, the entire description is itself a metaphor for a poem – 'typographic bushes' – the blackberries constituting the images growing thereon: the fruit of poetry.

I've taken the liberty of changing a couple of words in the quotation above. Brahic translates 'une famille rogue' as 'a rogue family', when *rogue* is actually French for 'haughty', a word which makes the image delightful as it is. (What exactly is a rogue family? A family of rogues? Have you ever *met* a whole family of rogues? Usually it's just thuggish teenage sons or an embezzling father who might be described as roguish. Haughty families, on the other hand, are ten a penny.) However, 'rogue' in English can also refer to a spoiled crop, which reflects Brahic's decision to write 'black, rose, khaki together on the bunch' as opposed to 'cluster' – which is the more accurate description of a spoiled blackberry. (It is, after all, grapes that grow in bunches.) Needless to say, this is nit-picking and it is unfortunate that this is one of my favourite of Ponge's early poems, meaning I've already completely assimilated an earlier American version into my mental furniture and feel quite attached to it. Elsewhere the directness and sensitivity of Brahic's translation is refreshing, and to finally see such previously untranslated works as the titular ode (along with over half of the prose poems in the book) is a great thing indeed. In any case, my carping is an indication of the difficulty of translating a writer whose tangents and imagery are inextricable from the language in which he wrote; every word could spark a debate. Any translation is really no less an achievement than Gilbert Adair's rendering Perec's *A Void* in English without the letter 'e'.

It is appropriate, for a writer so concerned with the contemplation of *things* that *Unfinished Ode to Mud* is such a lovely object in itself. CB Editions books are already starting to look iconic with their attractive, understated covers, satisfyingly compact size and weight. This excellent English edition of an underrated master of the prose poem makes them a press to celebrate.

62 (Spring 2009)

Rivers and Mountains

Editorial by *Tim Dooley*

In Jane Campion's atmospheric period romance, *Bright Star*, John Keats considers the critical response to his 1820 volume *Lamia, Isabella, The Eve of St. Agnes, and Other Poems* (surviving copies of which now sell for up to $30,000). Enthusiastic notices by friends and a few neutral reviews are placed alongside the long infamous character assassination of the quarterlies. Keats could weigh in the balance the notion that he would be 'among the English poets when I die' with a sense that his name was one 'writ in the water'. In a matter of decades Keats's reputation was secure. In the words of Tennyson's 'Ulysses', he had 'become a name'.

He had passed 'the test of time', a process touched on in a more recent context in Dennis O'Driscoll's collection of interviews with Seamus Heaney, *Stepping Stones* (reviewed in *Poetry London* last spring):

It's a matter of word of mouth between practitioners. It starts small, with the inner circle of contenders. Who's the good one out there? In poetry in particular, an ancient and sacred art, the word 'poet' still has an aura – that's why people want it so much. Maybe I'm talking idealistically; but I do believe that published poets have a responsibility to the unpublished poets in a way that novelists don't. It's a sacred charge; and that's why the selection process is independent almost of the marketing process or the reputation game.

Heaney's vision of a spontaneous election by the coming poet's peers is characteristically noble and generous. It's a process that the comparatively recent annual round of prizes and awards for poetry seeks to formalize, sometimes with mixed results. The fly in the ointment is, of course, that 'inner circle of contenders'. To some, outside the circle, this apparently natural process amounts to unelected electors fast-tracking figures formed in their own image, an accusation that can easily and sometimes accurately be caricatured as the envy of the less talented. As often in cases of mutual suspicion, those inside and outside may be prisoners of unhelpful metaphors. Poets should know better, yet remain captivated by figurative 'eminences', 'peaks' and (worst of all) 'career ladders'.

If topographical metaphors are needed perhaps they could be horizontal rather than vertical. In Auden's 'Journey to Iceland' a typographical error turned 'and the *poets* have names for the sea' to 'and the *ports* have names for the sea', an accidental improvement the poet was pleased to accept. At best the larger figures in our poetic landscape can be like ports, the arrival points to those outside the island, the starting point for excursions along the coast and into the hinterland of the art. So Carol Ann Duffy is using her laureateship to celebrate the wider work of poets, and Don Paterson, the newest recipient of the Queen's Gold Medal for Poetry, speaks of the honour giving him 'the permission to start working a lot harder' both on his own poetry, presumably, and in his work as an editor and encourager of new talent.

Poetry London takes delight in celebrating and engaging with the work of figures brave and well placed enough to traffic with a wider world. But they are only part of a rich network of creative practice, which can be traced and mapped out to find the secluded bays and riverside retreats of those who work with a lonelier integrity. So the reviews in this issue explore new work by Paterson, Gillian Clarke and Billy Collins and the work of very young poets with and without the support of major publishers. But we also cover collections by Thomas A. Clark, Ruth Stone and Samuel Menashe, who have pursued their craft quietly and little attended to over many years, achieving remarkable luminosity and authority. And it is a particular pleasure to publish an extended appreciation of the work of Selima Hill, whose strikingly independent voice and continuing creative exuberance place her surely 'among the English poets' of *at least* our time.

65 (Spring 2010)

A Church of Oranges and Flies

Helen Mort on *Selima Hill* and 'the female poem'

> *Can a very small grandmother*
> *alone in a room with a pigeon*
> *learn to fly?*

When I encounter a question like this, I know that it could only have been posed by Selima Hill, one of the most inventive and irrepressible poets writing today. Revisiting Hill's selected poems *Gloria* and her last collection *The Hat* in light of her new book *Fruitcake* is a dazzling, vaguely bewildering experience. *Fruitcake*'s title captures something of the essence of Hill's rich, enjoyable work, though it would, of course, be more accurate to liken Hill's poetry to a cake placed in the centre of the table at an afternoon tea party only for a large rabbit to leap out of the middle. *Fruitcake* is full of unexpected ingredients: inventive imagery, joyful punctuation and rapid about-turns. From the Daliesque world of a poem like 'Fresh Meat', where the narrator grows 'enormous breasts' that make her mother's bedroom 'smell of fresh meat', to the more controlled sequence, 'Nylon', cataloguing a childhood of aunts and tea and freedom, this is a collection of surprises. Just when we think we're following a poem, it wrong-foots us, throwing in 'a warble-fly... spelling trouble'.

These swerves are characteristic of a poet whose work over the last twenty-five years has always been a delightful and disconcerting experience. Nonetheless, Selima Hill's latest offering is a restrained, subtle collection, particularly when compared to her last book. Published in 2008, the short poems in *The Hat* put me in mind of a series of vivid snapshots: polaroids that seem to have been taken upside down, with the camera pointing at the photographer's left nipple or out of the window at the clouds. *The Hat* is about misunderstanding, betrayal, finding an identity; so it's apt that the poems in it should be difficult to follow, or sometimes trip the reader up with their awkward rhythm. An example is the tongue-twisting poem, 'The Darkness of her Meekness':

She rages in the darkness of her meekness
which they have installed in her as in stalls
while in the lounge her mother and her sisters
further their spectacular depressions.

The Hat is a collection that seeks to pull the rug from under our feet. Exclamation marks, used so often in Hill's work, have a kind of hysterical effect in these poems rather than an exuberant one. It is a book populated by unreliable narrators who describe 'Articulate Serrations' and 'The Kind of Neck People Want To Strangle'. *Fruitcake* has a contrasting tone. Composed of four sequences that all explore different facets of motherhood, Hill's latest collection brings together spare poems that cover a huge amount of ground. Flies are a recurring motif (a woman in 'Bunker Sacks' wears 'a dressing gown of flies') and the poems themselves have something of a swarming effect, bombarding us with surprising lines:

Anything alive
makes her nervous –

visitors, their flowers,
the endless flies,

and, dying
in my little muslin living room,

me
and my unmanageable head.

('Nervousness')

Hill is an effortlessly original poet. A glance through the titles in *Gloria: Selected Poems* would be enough in itself to confirm this, revealing such gems as 'Eating Chocolates in the Dark', 'Much Against Everyone's Advice', 'A Nightdress Sprinkled with Fish Scales', 'A Day in the Life of your Suitcase', and 'Hundreds of Letters to Hundreds of Naked Men', not to mention her celebrated 2002 sequence *Portrait of My Lover as a Horse* – typically of Hill, the book contains portraits of her lover as virtually everything (ash, a dead fish, her late father's suit, her ex-lover) *except* a horse. *Gloria* showcases the dazzling range of her work from the simple, brilliantly observed narrative of a poem like 'Dewpond and Black Drainpipes' (from her first collection, published in 1984) to the bizarre cataloguing of 'Our Lady of Meat' (from *A Little Book of Meat*, 1993). I was reminded of Hill's clarity of observation as well as her originality: *Bunny* (2001) is a collection full of perfect images. The night sky 'carries stars between its teeth / like pins in the teeth of a woman / designing a habit'. Thunder is 'a mother made of waterfalls'. Hill's is a strange and disembodied poetry, though it draws so strongly on the physical. She's a writer whose work is rooted in sensation, but who rapidly departs from it, making imaginative leaps that other poets might fear. The nature of connection in her work is encapsulated by the witty 'North Carolina':

Everything about you's a bit like me –
in the same way that North Carolina's a bit like
   Ribena
but rhymes with Vagina, which is nearly the
   same,
but much darker –
brutal and sweet like disease,
sweet as an asphalt dealer.

It's difficult to begin to describe Selima Hill's poetry, such is its scale and scope. Perhaps that's why it's tempting for reviewers to look at it through the lens of feminism or femininity. Writing in the *Guardian* in 2008, Fiona Sampson said of Hill:

Beside the ever-ready bodies consentingly sexualized by many of our younger women poets, Hill's explorations of femininity's conflicted backstory are sophisticated and multifaceted, their strategies strengthened by her use of book-length series of poems.

It's an interesting contrast to draw between Hill's work and the apparently 'sexualized' poetry of other writers, but one that is slightly reductive. Hill's work seems too varied in scope to be set against anyone else's – individual poems from *Gloria* could be set against each other – and her approach to femininity too complex to be isolated from her work as a whole.

Equally, one wonders, what this category of 'sexualized' poetry really is. Which writers and which poems?

A recent debate at the Aldeburgh Festival with Jo Shapcott, Annie Freud and Maureen Duffy discussed the nature of 'the female poem' and provoked questions about whether such a term is useful or not, or whether 'the poet can be moved along a continuum of femininity and masculinity in poems to produce the effects or characters needed'. Talking about 'female poetry' offers us a convenient way of approaching the difficulty of writing about subjective, conflicting experiences. It's unfortunate that in many cases, it tends to be the main lens through which a poet's work comes to be viewed and reviewed. Certainly, Selima Hill often explores subjective experiences of being female, and does so with her characteristic blend of wit and bleak humour. The way she views sex in poems like 'The Girl' and 'Tower', alternates between fascination and boredom: 'sex to me is like the violin'. *Red Roses* (2006) is a brutal evocation of feelings of powerlessness. Men are referred to as 'other', as 'they' or 'them':

Down between our little thighs their mouths
chomp and chew us like the mouths of dogs;
[...]
they ram themselves with thumps between our
   thighs
and pour with sweat, like tipped-up Golden
   Syrup tins.

('They Ram Themselves With
Thumps Between Our Thighs')

The poems explore violence, sex and household routine, making the patterns we live by seem entirely absurd; Hill, of course, is the master of the absurd, holding up a kind of funhouse mirror to the reader, throwing back a distorted image, tragic and comical in equal measure, almost unrecognizable, capturing our essence all the same. The issue of motherhood is the preoccupation in *Fruitcake* and to me the most powerful sequence in the book was the dark 'Bunker Sacks' about the shock of being a young mother. These are dense, uncompromising poems, exploring helplessness and responsibility. 'It's easy to be weak when you're weak', the narrator tells us. The sequence ends with the grotesque image of women hacking a baby to pieces before turning on each other. Ironically, the myriad of perspectives Hill manages to explore within her work defies the idea of 'the female poem'.

I would argue that there's another equally important strand running through her work, that of religion, particularly ideas of guilt and shame. In her originality, Hill can be seen as a kind of Blakean poet of revelation. I was particularly interested in the echoes of Blake's 'O Rose thou art sick' in 'Queenio': 'lust has turned her hidden milk to bone'. Her work is obsessed with the forbidden. Perhaps this is why its language is so daring, her images so off-kilter, testing the boundaries of what we will follow. In the poem 'Lust' she puts it thus:

> lust
> like pessaries
> that glide along my veins
> like gilded lozenges...

Elsewhere in 'Desire's a Desire', lust 'taunts...like the muzzle of a gun' or 'nuzzles...like fat dogs'. The poem concludes 'my only desire's a desire / to be free from desire'. When she writes about adolescence, it's often in these terms, viewed through the notion of sin or of repressed desires. In 'Little Sisters', she describes 'girls growing up into women / without knowing why'. Mystery is a potent theme in Hill's work, and it often relates to guilt and knowledge, the concept of original sin. These are poems of obsession, freedom and taboo. One of Hill's most intriguing poems is 'Selima Selima', published in *Aeroplanes of the World* (1994). If one of Hill's motifs is visual art and the portrait, can this be regarded as a kind of self-portrait? Hill asks 'Where does shame come from?' and concludes:

> It comes from my name.
> Selima, Selima.
> My father gave it to me.

An equally important thread is the fear of being touched. Her narrators often melt like snow or shatter like glass when touched (a metaphor for how to read Hill's poems: try to interrogate them too closely and they might break). In the poem 'No-one' she describes how 'his fingertips caress me / like a knife'. It's as if, by exploring the surreal, Hill is testing the idea of whether there is any logic to the world, a creator with grand design. Take the poem 'Articulate Serrations' in *The Hat*:

> Articulate serrations of cracked skulls
> tell us God
> has been here before us,
> or something has,
> and might come again –
> something with a little spade or scalpel
> whose blades are rays
> and know the darkness needs them.

Hill is fascinated by the idea of creation and control, and her poems about sex and motherhood could equally be seen through this lens rather than in terms of some concept of 'the female poem'.

Her poem 'What Do I Really Believe' is a kind of treatise, an attempt to engage with the idea of a shaping force or grand narrative. It's appropriate that what Hill claims to truly believe in this poem is, in a sense, imagery and language itself. The poem is a celebration of the visual, the musical, the bizarre. Ultimately, it is a celebration of language:

> I believe that antithesis and hyperboles
> dilate like slowly eaten fruit;

> I believe that when a man takes long, deep breaths
> he is trying not to prematurely ejaculate.

It brings to mind something that Hill herself says in an interview with Lidia Vianu in 2006:

> Poets in their poems feel safe. And when we feel safe we feel free. Free to love. To trust our reader. To forgive our tormentors. To be tender. To meet God, and camels and suitcases and dogs and lettuces... 'If you have a hammer, everything begins to look like a nail' (Nietzsche). If you are a

poet, everything begins to look beautiful! I don't mean you have to like it (it, the world, everything) – but you do have to love it. This is what my poetry can say. All poetry is love poetry. We sit on God's velvet cushion. We are God's spies! I would rather be good than happy.

It's this dialogue between freedom and restriction in her work that gives Hill's poetry much of its power. Her response to the tyranny of the forbidden is to embrace language: the best vehicle we have for exploring the bizarre taboos and norms of the world and, in doing so, challenging them. Selima Hill's quasi-religious poetry is a broad church – one that's built on her distinctive linguistic architecture: packed with oranges, swarming with flies.

65 (Spring 2010)

Plain Heaven and the Sound of Truth

George Szirtes on *Peter Porter*'s art of seriousness

It was Paul Verlaine, a poet Peter Porter didn't particularly like, who promised to take eloquence and wring its neck. But what was eloquence? What indeed was poetry? The first four lines of 'The Lying Art' show a distinct scepticism about the values claimed for it:

It is all rhetoric rich as wedding cake
And promising the same bleak tears
When what was asked for but not recognized
Shows its true face after a thousand breakfasts...

Peter Porter spent much of his life with his hands round the neck of rhetoric. That was his great strength. Time after time he despaired of poetry, or at least of its idealization. He pursued the hopelessness of poetic ambition from 'The Great Poet Comes Here in Winter' (his early dramatic monologue about Rilke that begins 'Frau Antonia is a cabbage: / If I were a grub I'd eat a hole in her') through to the late poem, 'Tasso's Oak', where he writes:

The fault was Poetry's, those worlds which
  clashed
Like blades but never joined the field, the sound
Of truth but bearing no true weight,

Why should scepticism be a strength? The answer lies in the phrase, 'the sound of truth but bearing no true weight'. It is truth that matters. It is the care for truth, the demand for it that led him to doubt the claims of 'the lying art'. The tension between distrust and its object lies at the heart of Porter's entire enterprise. His true interlocutor is God, the god of death and art. So it was in 'Forefathers' View of Failure', the first poem of *The Rest on the Flight* – this vast four-hundred-page selection from his poems. It was the god of those he first knew: 'Men with religion as their best technique / Who built bush churches six days a week'. Those churches were built of 'weatherboard' and were 'bleached white'. Like the War Memorial, also mentioned in the poem, they led eyes to 'a plain Heaven'. An ironic distance is maintained between the poet and the church builders, his forefathers, but they are the plain heaven ghosts in the machinery of his imagination. Like Marianne Moore, like Peter Porter, *they too* distrusted poetry.

All the same – and this is the point – for someone who distrusted poetry so much, he wrote a great deal of it and that great deal comprises a great deal. That is because unlike a sceptic who shrugs, raises his eyebrow and has ever less to say, Porter possessed a restless, almost volcanic curiosity. Anyone who ever spent time in his company as I did, particularly as a young poet to whom he was typically generous, cannot fail to speak about his encyclopaedic reading and conversation. The last time I saw him he was in his chair reading a book of verse. 'I have read forty pages of this without coming across a memorable line', were his first words. Mine might have been, 'And yet you are still reading'. He absorbed everything, listened to everything, looked at everything, eager to examine and know the nature of it. The poet, regarded first as a turncoat then as a returning master in his home country Australia, filled his mind with the history and productions of the Old World, absorbing its pretensions, voluptuousness, decrepitude, power, ambition and grandeur almost by way of inoculating himself against it, while becoming of it. The monuments of European culture were both glories and puzzles. Chiefly, I believe, they spoke to him of vanity and mortality, a plain heaven transfigured into a Baroque ceiling by, say, Andrea Pozzo. Those pastoral scenes in Piero di Cosimo or Lorenzo Lotto were displacements of the forefathers' new land where 'the transplanted grasses root, / Waving as silkily as through old falling soot'.

Back in the early Sixties there was God, there was art, there was history and there was London: the London of copywriting and early satires like 'A Consumer's Report', 'The World of Simon Raven' and 'John Marston Advises Anger', which are really only partly satires. A comic melancholia haunts them: a sense that not only the Australian landscape but Porter himself was being displaced. He was by this time a member of The Group along with Peter Redgrove, Alan Brownjohn and Martin Bell, and was one of its leading lights. Not precisely the poetic equivalents of Osborne's angry young men, Group members were nevertheless class-combative and determined to address the world, to point out its hypocrisies, and to cut up rough if need be. Porter was not going to forget the obligations of plain heaven. As the speaker of the dramatic monologue, Fredric II of Prussia, reminds himself, in 'Soliloquy at Potsdam':

There are always the poor –
Getting themselves born in crowded houses.
Feeding on the parish, losing their teeth early
And learning to dodge blows...
('Forefathers' View of Failure')

In the poem Fredric goes on to consider his court composer Johann Joachim Quantz, weighing three sonatas against the march of a hundred regiments. That was the tension: the balance between Brisbane, Porter's birthplace in 1929, and Bayswater. Quantz would cut it in London but Quantz had a lot to answer for.

So it continued on ever-new ground: the same battles and fascinations, in ever-new corners of the cultural map (a map he would consider a spiritual map), in a craft so fragile it was always threatening to sink. There is a later parody of Harold Bloom's *The Western Canon* titled 'The Western Canoe'. A man may think he is paddling his own but must carry the list of approved passengers: George Steiner, the Theory Fairy, the Gulf War, Gibbon, Dickens, the Eco Pool, the Lady Murasaki, not to forget Harold Bloom himself. And Quantz is there, and Fredric II with his poor bloody armies. All this would be intolerable name-dropping if we were not convinced that he had read, listened and looked at every item in the canoe and that it had mattered. But we *are* so convinced, because it clearly did and does matter. Italian Renaissance art is of vital importance. German music and philosophy are integral to life. The Latins and Greeks are the life-blood of Bayswater Road.

What have they to do with us? Everything. It is not that they must be taken seriously, meaning solemnly. It is not because they are the best that has been thought. It is not because they do so civilize a man. It is certainly not for the sake of after-dinner conversation. It is because truth matters. It is because Brisbane exists. This passionate, ironic flood of ideas carries Porter through some twenty books. Nor does he ever tire. Not every poem is deathless, not every line laden with ore; or rather, death itself is the ore. Nevertheless he turns a smart line when he feels like it, because the ex-copywriter knew a thing or two about hook-lines. Paradoxically, though the figure of Porter the poet is so imposing that it will continue to fascinate and expand, the book by which he might best survive in terms of the totality of individual poems, his best loved book, is his least characteristic work: *The Cost of Seriousness*, published in 1978 after the death by suicide of his first wife, Jannice Henry. *The Cost of Seriousness* is his most personal book, and certainly his most autobiographical. Here the man has stepped out of his canoe and stands forlornly on the banks of the river, the Lethe, the Acheron, the Styx. The clutter of civilization does not desert him but almost everything else does. His response is in the title poem, the figure naked, clad only in art:

Once more I come to the white page of art
    to discover what I know

and what I presume I feel
about those forgettable objects words
We begin with penalties:
the cost of seriousness will be death...

In poem after poem there he anatomizes art, seeking both consolation and desolation. Even nakedness is an art that must be mastered, he learns, never having loved nakedness. He cannot know naked feeling; he must, as he says, *presume* what he feels. That, paradoxically, *is* the nakedness.

The self appears in Porter's work; it is never absent. It's in the voice, the pace, the subject matter, the humour. Porter was, after all, an Auden man but his God was sterner, more puritan than Auden's. Porter's God was guilty by way of non-existence, just as his own speech was guilty by way of silence. For his conventional Anglican funeral Peter Porter asked that Psalm Thirty-nine be read. It begins:

> I said, I will take heed to my ways, that I sin not with my tongue: I will keep my mouth with a bridle, while the wicked is before me.
> I was dumb with silence, I held my peace, *even* from good; and my sorrow was stirred.
> My heart was hot within me, while I was musing the fire burned: *then* spake I with my tongue,
> LORD, make me to know mine end, and the measure of my days, what it *is*; *that* I may know how frail I *am*.

This belongs with the plain heaven of the crowded houses: more Brisbane than Bayswater. Auden was never Brisbane. Porter's laughter, considering the god in question, was blacker and more bitter. The laughter was in the bones and the bones were many.

67 (Autumn 2010)

Truth and Dare: An Interview

Kathryn Maris talks to *Christopher Reid* on the publication of his *Selected Poems* about his willingness to 'try anything'

Kathryn Maris: What was your experience of putting together a *Selected Poems*?

Christopher Reid: I had to be coaxed into it by Paul Keegan, my editor at Faber and Faber, who, ten years ago or more, suggested I might put a *Selected* together. At the time I was reluctant – I don't have that retrospective urge, really. But then I got the big prize last year and I thought, 'Come on, I've got to do it. There's no point in being precious'. And in the end it wasn't so painful, going back and rereading and coming to judgments about old work.

KM: What kind of judgments did you make?

CR: Numerous. How much to put in was a crucial one. First of all I made a much longer book. But the centre of gravity was wrong; it felt out of balance. In the end I think it was for the health of the book that I cut it sharply back.

KM: The first poem in your Selected, 'Arcadia', which is also the title of your first collection, takes a child's picture as its starting point. Can you tell me a bit about your childhood – you were born in Hong Kong – and the impact poetry had on you in your early years?

CR: The Hong Kong part was over by the time I was four. My parents came to this country, briefly, at that stage, so my memories of Hong Kong are very vague and probably more photographic than direct. My parents weren't especially bookish, but one of the books they had around the house was a volume of selections from the magazine *Punch*, which I loved for the cartoons. Then I started to notice that there were these arrangements of words in the corners of some of the pages. They were poems, little *vers de société* of the kind that *Punch* in the 1950s used to publish. I found the actual volume the other day, in a secondhand bookshop, and bought it as souvenir. But it's quite hard to be amused by it now. At the time, though, I was enchanted. I thought, 'Gosh, you can play around with words like this, can you?' and started doing so myself.

KM: Was memorizing poems part of your education?

CR: It was. I was sent to a prep school – a boarding school – because my parents went away again to live abroad: not back to Hong Kong, but the Middle East. And so my brother and I were parked at boarding school. It was a very old-fashioned boys' education including at an early age Latin and French, Greek later. And, yes, the English teachers required us to learn verses: bits of Shakespeare, bits of Keats, bits of Henry Newbolt.

KM: One of things you are known for is the Martian movement, a metaphor-driven poetry that emphasized the defamiliarization of the ordinary and the domestic. Can you tell me how it was started and who was involved?

CR: There was never any 'Martian school'. That was a kind of fiction, an invention of James Fenton's, who wrote a review of my first book and Craig Raine's second. Craig was very helpful to me in my growth as a poet and, in the early days, he and I used to swap poems and pronounce on them. Craig was a very tough critic and therefore an inspiring teacher. I guess it was largely through his predilection for the kind of metaphor that you just described that I got interested in writing like that. So to that extent he egged me on and I followed. But there was never any conscious school or doctrine or manifesto. Nothing of that kind. We were just pleasing ourselves, entertaining each other.

KM: So you weren't consciously reacting against anything?

CR: I think we thought we were reacting against a prevalent dullness in English poetry, as represented mainly by The Movement. But in truth I don't remember reading much poetry by The Movement,

so I was probably reacting against something I'd imagined rather than something that was real.

KM: Were the Modernists important for you, in particular Ezra Pound and his mandate to 'make it new'? Because it seems as though that is what you were doing.

CR: The Modernists were hugely important, in particular Eliot and Stevens. Pound less so, though I liked his early lyrics a great deal. More than that, when I was a student at Oxford, I wasn't reading much contemporary British poetry, but I was buying that wonderful series Penguin put out, of Modern European Poets. So poetry from Poland, and what was Yugoslavia, and what was Czechoslovakia, and what was the USSR – they were the stuff I knew about. I'd read much more of Zbigniew Herbert than I had of Philip Larkin.

KM: How do the 'Martian' poems stand up now?

CR: Some of mine are awful, but I'm quite pleased with others. They have a sort of reckless energy.

KM: When I was a schoolgirl in America, my English teacher talked about 'Martian Poetry'. It was known internationally.

CR: Well, it's funny, that. I was aware of fame spreading abroad and I got invited to a few foreign conferences on the strength of it. But there was no huge impact at home. The sales of my early books were pitifully small.

KM: Craig Raine once said you have an impeccable ear for breaking a line. What do you consider your strengths as a poet?

CR: Oh, I don't know. Possibly my strength is that I'll try anything.

KM: Critics who reviewed your book *Arcadia* described you as 'unfeeling'. Was that commonly said about your early work?

CR: It's still said. I had a selected poems (*Mermaids Explained*) out in America about ten years ago. It got a review in the *New York Times* by somebody who more or less said that it was all to do with fancy wordplay, hard-hearted and shallow. Not quite how I see it.

KM: Has your work become more sentimental in recent years? Larkin said he didn't understand the word 'sentimentality' and thought that Dylan Thomas's definition of an alcoholic – 'a man you don't like who drinks as much as you do' – could be applied to 'sentimental': 'someone you don't like who feels as much as you do'. How do you view sentimentality?

CR: Larkin also said somewhere that the transaction between writer and reader is that you, as the writer, feel something, and you want the reader to feel the same thing. That's more or less my recipe. Maybe sometimes sentimentality – the corruption of sentiment – does creep into it. But I'd hope not. I was very aware when I was writing *A Scattering* that sentimentality was the trap.

KM: Let's play a game of Either/Or. Which is the more important component of a poem: wit or imagination?

CR: I think more about imagination than I do about wit – if by imagination you mean some quality of sympathy with whatever thing you're trying to get at.

KM: A poem's technique or a poem's idea?

CR: They have to be working absolutely together.

KM: Being daring or being in control?

CR: Being daring, definitely.

KM: Truth or inventiveness?

CR: Inventiveness is really a means at getting at the truth. That's the intention at any rate.

KM: *Katerina Brac*, your third collection, is a pseudo-translation of an invented Eastern European poet. And your fourth collection, *In The Echoey Tunnel*, contains a long poem ('Memres of Alfred Stoker') in which you take on the persona of an old man reflecting on his strange childhood. What was the attraction of assuming different voices? Was it liberating?

CR: Yes. In the case of Katerina it was that I'd been writing, after my first two books, more poems and then immediately throwing them away, because they seemed to me stuck in self-imitation and not advancing the game at all. And this went on for a couple of years. Then I had the bright idea that the best way not to sound like myself was to write somebody else's poems for them. So I took an imaginative holiday to a distant part of the world and found *Katerina Brac*.

KM: Did the fact that you'd done so much reading of Eastern European poetries at university have any bearing on your choice of Katerina?

CR: I'm sure it did. Of course, one of the things that is problematic about reading foreign poetry, from a language you don't have, is that you're taking a great deal on trust, and the person you're trusting is the translator. So I had a sense that I knew what a translator's voice was more clearly than I knew the voices of certain Eastern European poets. What I was trying to catch in Katerina's poems was the hint that behind my inadequate English there was something rather rich and wonderful to which the reader lacked direct access but which was nonetheless present as a kind of ghost or intuition.

KM: In your collection *Mr Mouth*, you invent yet another character, but this eponymous protagonist, who is generally referred to in the third person, seems to be a metaphor or device. Were these poems written as a way out of silence? Did Mr Mouth become your mouthpiece?

CR: I had the idea for *Mr Mouth* when, in the notebook I used to keep in those days, I wrote down the enigmatic words 'Mr Mouth'. This seemed to me rather potent, though I couldn't yet tell how. Then a couple of years later I was editing Ted Hughes's letters and the words came to life. Somebody else noticed it more quickly than I did when I showed them the poems. They said, 'I can see what you're doing: it's your version of *Crow*'. Which hadn't been my conscious intention, though probably Ted's great, wild book had given me licence to go on a romp of my own. Obviously they're utterly different: *Crow* is dark, tragic, apocalyptic, about all the finally essential things, whereas Mr Mouth is constantly dodging out of the way and coming up with a clever comment rather than an authentic response. So he is a kind of comic inversion, maybe, of *Crow*. But I hadn't plotted it like that. Just one summer, whilst I was in the middle of editing the letters, I thought 'I must write something and enjoy myself', and that was the result.

KM: Do you have a favourite Ted Hughes collection?

CR: *Crow* is one of my favourites. And I love *River*. But my admiration for Ted spreads evenly across most of his volumes.

KM: What was it like editing Ted Hughes?

CR: Marvellous. He was so stimulating, full of surprises, very genial and candid. Being in his company was always fun. And receiving his phone calls and letters. Tremendous.

KM: And the experience of editing his letters?

CR: That was marvellous. I knew it would be. I actually suggested to Carol Hughes, his widow, at an early stage, that the thing that would most change public understanding of Ted would be a collection of his letters. Because I'd received a fair number myself and knew that the writer of those letters was out of sight for most people – I mean the Ted who was constantly encouraging you, interested in you, always asking questions, totally direct and without any side whatsoever. I thought 'That's the Ted Hughes that people ought to know about'. And there it was in abundance as I gathered the material.

KM: Seamus Heaney said, 'I think poets shouldn't work too hard at other jobs, because I think if you commit a lot of your attention and your tension in another place, you close the receiving stations'. That doesn't appear to have been the case for you. You were poetry editor at Faber for several years and, before then, you worked on *Crafts*, the magazine of the Crafts Council. You were briefly a professor at the University of Hull and you also run a small press, Ondt & Gracehoper. How has your professional life interacted with your poetry?

CR: My main aim from the moment I left university was to avoid the sort of job that would be wholly involving and eat up my time and stop me from writing. So I've had occasional full-time employment, but very little. My job at the Crafts Council was full-time and that's why I only lasted two years. Faber employed me half-time, which was fine: I used to do two weeks in the office and then two weeks away. Inevitably you take work home – that's unavoidable – but somewhere in the middle of my two weeks off I would have time wholly to myself and that would allow me to keep going.

KM: Who were the poets you took on at Faber, and could you say something, briefly, about what you admired in each of them?

CR: That would be difficult.

KM: Can you name a few then?

CR: Simon Armitage, Don Paterson, Lavinia Greenlaw, Jamie McKendrick, August Kleinzahler, Charles Simic, the wonderful Katherine Pierpoint (I wish she would publish some more poems!), Maurice Riordan, Wisława Szymborska, a few others. And Fergus Allen. I'm delighted to have spotted him. They all stand for so many different virtues. What was I looking out for generally? Something distinctive, something that had authenticity. But I didn't have a template. I didn't have a platonic model of the Faber Poet that people had to match.

KM: Let's return to your own work. You published an attractive pamphlet called *Universes* under your own imprint of Ondt & Gracehoper which later became a full collection called *Expanded Universes* with Faber. Was it always your intention to develop *Universes* into a full collection?

CR: The reason I put *Universes* together was frustration. The maddening thing about being an editor at a place like Faber, and no doubt any bigger publishing firm, is that you're not in charge of every detail of the book as it passes through production and goes out into the world. In those days Faber printed on the most wretched paper and I found that hugely embarrassing, that great poets were being printed on rubbish stock, which turned jaundice-yellow the moment you opened the book. So I thought I must gratify the perfectionist in me and produce a little book of my own where everything would be exactly as I wanted it. I worked with Ron Costley who designs for Faber and has an immaculate eye. Just for the fun of it really – just a hobbyish exercise. I had no idea that I would go on to do other books. In the case of *Universes*, I had a bunch of poems ready and a quote from Alexander Calder that fitted (it provided both title and epigraph). Then in due course I wrote more poems that clustered around those initial ones and the result was *Expanded Universes*. But whenever I've done a book with Ondt & Gracehoper in recent times it's been – well, sometimes it's been because nobody else would publish the damn thing! – but really the major purpose has been to please myself by making something that I thought looked lovely.

KM: You've written quite a lot of children's poetry (published by Ondt & Gracehoper), none of which wound up in your Selected.

CR: Only for reasons of economy. And anyway I put Mr Mouth in, who pretty well represents that strain in me.

KM: Your three most recent collections, *Mr Mouth*, *A Scattering* and *The Song of Lunch* seem very different from your earlier collections, with *For And*

After (to my mind) a transitional collection. Were you aware of any shift in ambition? Or did external factors have a bearing on this change in scope?

CR: *Mr Mouth* was the first of the three and it came about as a break from working on Ted's letters. The idea was to have fun really, which I did, so much so that I had to make myself stop at a certain stage. It was a surprisingly fecund subject and I could have gone on endlessly, but a hundred and eleven poems was plenty. The second of those books was prompted by factors I could not have foretold: the death of my wife. If that's different, it's no doubt because I'd never had to confront that sort of subject matter before. And a lot of the book's qualities are Lucinda's qualities.

KM: Did you have any models for elegiac collections, for example Douglas Dunn's?

CR: No, I didn't really think about others. I had individual poems as models. They were all old, like Henry King's 'The Exequy'. Or there's the amazing poem by Ben Jonson about his son's death. None of the poems in *A Scattering* matches or resembles either, but they were reminders to me that if you're writing about grief you still have to rise to technical challenges, which are in fact essential to conveying the grief. There are lines in 'The Exequy' where, if you're reading the poem aloud, King can make tears start purely through artful touches in the versification. For example, in the couplet –

But hark! my pulse like a soft drum
Beats my approach, tells thee I come;

– where he adapts the stresses in the second line to the beat of a funeral march. It's an extraordinary moment, the very highest kind of writing in that vein.

KM: What other projects, besides your *Selected*, have you completed recently?

CR: I wrote some songs for the composer Colin Matthews ['Airs and Ditties of No Man's Land'].

They were performed at the BBC Proms in July 2011, with Ian Bostridge and Roderick Williams and the City of London Sinfonia – a thrilling experience. I'd love to do more of that sort of thing, but commissions don't exactly overwhelm me.

KM: What's next?

CR: I've just delivered a collection to Faber, which they'll bring out in about a year's time. The working title is *Nonsense* and it's got a couple of narrative poems in it, developments from what I started in *The Song of Lunch*. Then there are more unpublished poems beyond that, but they'll have to wait.

71 (Spring 2012)

O Sweet Frustrations!

Editorial by *Martha Kapos*

'I wonder if you read much foreign poetry?' Ian Hamilton once asked Philip Larkin. '*Foreign* poetry? No!' This interview was in 1964, and since then attitudes have changed. Now the shock of the foreign offers the possibility of seeing the world afresh from a viewpoint valued for the very fact that it stands at a surprising angle to our own. *Poetry Parnassus*, in which *Poetry London* is taking part, has invited 204 far-flung poets representing each country in the Olympics to break through their language barriers for an exuberant week at London's Southbank Centre of interaction, readings, translation, and general cultural unity.

The promise of an intimacy between languages is both bewildering and enthralling: a promise all the more compelling because it is held under the sign of a taboo – a taboo which places an insurmountable barrier in front of the translator. Once upon a time, we are told in *Genesis*, 'all the earth was one language and one set of words'. But the tower of Babel, which was to reach right up to heaven, was built with such an ecstatic sense of oneness, such an ideal of transparent communication that God clearly saw that it was beyond the human. In this respect the destruction of the tower and the scattering of humanity into different languages and cultures has the force of a second fall. Translation is condemned to imperfection; it is a suffering in exile; the translator is always attempting something that is both promised and denied as if it were a return to Eden. Robert Frost spoke of the unhappiness we should properly feel when reading translated poetry because what in fact was lost in translation was poetry itself.

The language of loss is a commonplace in discussions of poetry translation. 'One can go across a border naked,' wrote Karl Kraus, 'but not without one's skin. For, unlike clothes, one cannot acquire a new skin'. Walter Benjamin in *The Task of the Translator* uses the same images: 'While content and language form a certain unity, like a fruit and its skin, the language of translation envelops its content like a royal robe with ample folds' and it remains 'unsuited to its content, overpowering and alien'.

Yet it is the very unity of the fruit and its skin in the original that, according to Benjamin, fascinates and fixes the translator in his task. The desire of the translator is to achieve an intimate closeness to the original, to touch almost with a lover's intensity the area of the poem where its language and content are so tightly fused as to be inseparable. Even while the barriers between one's own language and that of the original ensure that meaning shifts, changes and eludes, the translator goes in longing pursuit as if it were the beloved itself. Figures of the erotic come irresistibly to mind: the relation of the translator to the original as 'faithful' or 'free' being only one example.

Perhaps it's also the roundness in the fruit/skin image that reminds me, at this point, of Aristophanes' account in Plato's *Symposium* of the origin of the sexes – a story of the fall in another form. Aristophanes, the comic poet, tells the conference of philosophers with a straight face that human beings were once round organisms composed of two people fused together into one complete sphere. Rolling around everywhere together they achieved perfect happiness. But in their ecstasy they threatened to roll right to the top of Olympus, whereupon Zeus chopped each of them in two. From which point onwards, Aristophanes might say, if this were an image of translation, the poet is left hunting for a completion that the poem in the original promises, but can never absolutely supply. It is only to be found in the reunion of the two halves: the complex and intimate relationship of mingling and opposition explored between two poets separated by their languages. 'O sweet frustrations!' Richard Wilbur wrote, 'We shall be back for more'.

72 (Summer 2012)

A *Fin de Siècle* Mahon

Patrick McGuinness on Derek Mahon's slippery conclusions

'*Tous les mégots de siècles se ressemblent*', wrote Huysmans in *Against Nature*, the 1884 novel that became the Decadent bible. A rough translation would be 'every century's butt-ends look the same'. The Mahon of the 1990s, of *The Hudson Letter* (here renamed 'New York Time') and *The Yellow Book* (here clunkingly retitled 'Decadence'), made much of the resemblance between his own *fin de siècle* and the '*mégot*' of the nineteenth century. In that sense there also seemed to be something symbolic about bringing out a *Collected* in 1999, on the centennial – on the millennial – cusp. But if there are plenty of false starts in poetry, there are also plenty of false endings, as the first *Collected* proved.

Mahon's 'New' *Collected* is almost a hundred pages longer, even with the omission of several important poems, including 'A Kensington Notebook', and all but a few of his versions and translations (published separately as *Raw Material*). Also missing are the *faux* translations of a Hindi poet, Gopal Singh, invented for *An Autumn Wind*. This new edition shows Mahon's capacity for off-key self-editing, but also his well-documented penchant for wasteful and infelicitous revisions. Like the first *Collected*, this book is unsignposted. Though chronological, the table of contents does not divide the work into volumes. The gaps between collec-

tions, a year or two here, a decade or so there, are collapsed, books wash into and out of each other like outlines in a watercolour. There's a certain logic to that; at nearly four hundred pages, this *Collected* feels both monumental and oddly fluid. Some may find this disorientating, but it is fitting enough for a poet who comes in waves rather than segments.

Seasoned finisecularists would in any case have realized that if Mahon knew his endings, he'd be back soon enough with a new one, because if there's one thing a *fin de siècle* is rarely about, it's the '*fin*'. The last decade or so has been one of Mahon's most productive, with *Harbour Lights* in 2005, *Life on Earth* in 2009, and *An Autumn Wind* a year later, as well as a number of adaptations, translations and *plaquettes*. This makes a kind of sense, as Mahon's 'Yellow Book' pose – part-languid observer of a rising tide of Celtic Tiger tat, part ironic Luddite (preferring, in one poem, the fur on the edge of the typewritten letter to the computer screen) – was never really about endings and exhaustion, but about what could be made, lyrically, from what he called 'the forest of intertexuality' ('Hangover Square'). Mahon has always been in search of the clearing in the intertextual forest, and managed to make poems even when there were no clearings to be found. In this respect he is a great *fin de siècle* writer, because, where other poets might simply have walked away, rebelled, or tried to start afresh, he always turns that choking surfeit of models and examples to his advantage. There are no clean slates, and one thing Mahon has kept faith with from his earliest work is this sense of the crowdedness of the terrain.

It's not just about being Ireland's 'most European' or 'most French' or 'most cosmopolitan' poet, since these phrases don't tell us much about Mahon, and take criticism of his poetry in predictable directions. It's more about the way in which Mahon negotiates cultural saturation, how he plays his game of constantly sorting the gold from the detritus, weighing them up, and finishes up by keeping both. This is why there are so many landmarks in his poems, what Baudelaire called 'Phares' or Lighthouses, by whom the artist navigates, but against whom he also risks shipwreck: other writers, painters, poets, the ancients and the moderns, and all their accumulation of great works and monuments. But there's also a lot of, well… rubbish: trash, junk, scraps, cast-offs, lost things: a clutter in search of a context, and his poems give voice to that too. Mahon knows that a culture's dustbin is the double of its library, its disused shed the forgotten twin of its museum.

The Mahon of the 1990s seemed to be all about lists and inventories and enumerations, as if telling a rosary of never-quite-last things. But already in a poem from the 1970s, 'Beyond Howth Head', he described himself as

> rehearsing for the *fin de siècle*
> gruff jeremiads to redirect
> lost youth into the knacker's yard
> of humanistic self-regard.

A great deal of Mahon is, in an appropriately French vein, poetry about what it is to be a poet, with all the grandeur and prestigious futility that implies. There was an irony in earlier Mahon about the 'role' of 'the poet'; and also a kind of charm. If he was jaded, he was at least freshly jaded – as he writes in 'Sunday Morning', he flies

> The private kite of poetry –
> a sort of winged sandwich board
> El-Grecoed to receive the word;
> an airborne, tremulous brochure
> proclaiming that the end is near.

The analogy is clever, surprising, but stays just this side of the laboured. It's more Laforgue than Huysmans.

Mahon has his totemic times and places: in 'Kensington Notebook' it's the Modernist London of Pound and Ford Madox Ford, Hulme and Eliot. In 'The Yellow Book' it's the Dublin-Paris axis of Irish writers who, as Pound put it, had 'gone to school on the French': Yeats, Synge, George Moore. But it's also about their forgotten contemporaries, the English 'poètes maudits' like Dowson and Symons and Lionel Johnson. And there's something defiantly *niche* about invoking Richard le Gallienne in order to situate oneself in the 1990s, playing out one's own

anxieties about posterity, about legacy, about reputation, but distancing them by casting them in period costume. The cast of second- and third-order characters make interesting foils for the greater presences such as Yeats and Synge, but Mahon's point is that they're all connected. It's where he's at his most Poundian too: interested less in the big names aspicated by the canon than in the interaction of people and energies, the ambience and atmosphere of a period. What Pound called 'the tone of the time'.

Mahon concentrates on productive in-betweenness and on the stimulations of exile – Ovid in Tomis, Pound in Kensington, Synge in Paris – but also on the meeting-places and meeting-moments of different cultures. This gives sequences like 'Decadence' and 'New York Time' an occasionally supine, name-dropping smugness that some critics objected to, especially when it came with an accompanying pose of weary superiority:

> I sit here like Domitian in a hecatomb of dead flies,
> an armchair explorer in an era of cheap flight.

Mahon's Des Esseintes persona, with his misanthropic elitism, has something of de Maistre's *Voyage Around My Room* about him too: an attempt to come to terms with the Great Indoors that constitutes a literary inheritance. As for the Great Outdoors, I've always thought Mahon's poems about nature have a sense of surprise about them, as if he's just put his book down, walked out, and found that the sea, the trees, the mountains are – yes, look! – still there. Mahon's poems about places – his coasts and mountains, his seascapes and landscapes – seem to me just as mediated as his poems about paintings. Can one be ekphrastic about Nature? I don't know, but Mahon's Nature feels looked at as if it were a picture of Nature. This is what makes his poems about the natural world interesting, unlike poems such as 'World Trade Talks', where he tries out some eco-abstractions about global warming and the despoliation of natural resources.

Some found 1990s Mahon flippant and self-regarding, his answer to the enormous social and economic changes in Ireland and Europe little more than churlishness and abdication. What also contributed to the monotony of those books was their delivery: heavy couplets dragging themselves from rhyme to rhyme, their virtuosity all reflex and no reflection. But there was another way of looking at those poems, and that was to think of them as fugues on the idea of originality, on the very possibility of originality in a saturated culture – certainly this was the paradox of the late nineteenth-century writers: that what was most original about them was the fear that there was no margin left to be original. That was always a Mahonian anxiety, and we see it in his earliest work. It was a brave thing to face up to then, and it seemed to me to remain so in the 1990s. To revisit that theme as Mahon did in the late twentieth century, with its implied culture- and situation-rhymes between two *fins de siècle*, was to add a third instalment to the double bluff of literary impotence. Is this what he meant, in 'Hangover Square', by 'surviving even beyond the age of irony / to the point where the old stuff comes round again'? Maybe. Either way, Mahon's triple bluff – whereby one returns to the possibility of originality by a kind of *via negativa* of repetition and paralysis – bypassed many critics, who saw him as a monomaniacal grouch chasing a single idea across metres of typewriter ribbon.

For me, there was something searching and profound about the way those books meditated on Time and memory, on what stays and what goes, and on the way culture somehow composts down into a mulch you can live on even though it smells of decay. Perhaps *because* it smells of decay. Mahon's endings were imbricated with beginnings, and his 1990s poems continually seemed to ask whether we were caught in a cycle or stuck in a decline. The answer appeared to be: both. We were in Beckettian Time – stasis braided around degradation – and though there was nothing minimalist about Mahon, he had Beckett's compulsive rephrasing itch, the constant iteration, reiteration and (here comes the redemptive triple-bluff) re-reiteration, whereby, by dint of repetition, one says something new for the first time once again. And in any case, even those airless, inert couplets of his had a tamped-down monotony, kneading the words into predictability, and there was always enough deadpan and savagery to liven things up. It's hard not to admire a poem with lines like 'Today is the first day of the rest of your life? / Tell that to your liver, tell that to your ex-wife'.

There was relief when Mahon came up with something more wholeseome perhaps, but also more muscularly late-Yeatsian, with *Harbour Lights* and the poems of the 2000s. The recent poems have been more limber, less clogged up; still allusive but less freighted with cultural cargo. The title poem of *Harbour Lights* promised, with its echo of Mallarmé, another fugue on urbane impotence – 'The flesh is weary and I've read the books' – but the end of the poem is much more open and hopeful. If this is what we want – and I think I still prefer Mahon's Yellow Nineties – then poems like this are better able to integrate personal with collective experience than those of the previous decade. Recent poems such as 'Sand Studies', 'Somewhere the Wave' and 'Thunder Shower' are beautifully modulated, elemental poems about the inner and the outer worlds, and seem to come from a different place. Some of the poems even mention package holiday destinations such as Tenerife and Lanzarote, so perhaps our armchair traveller has deigned to take Ryanair after all. The misanthropy has abated too.

Criticism generally attributes this sort of thing to 'late style', but that's to miss the point that Mahon came to late style pretty early on. From the start he had this tendency, prevalent among the Northern Irish poets, to write the middle-aged-sounding letter to another poet. The 'Epistle to…' format tended to assert poetic community. It's the kind of trope some academic will one day call 'performing poetivity'. For poems as awkward as 'The Yaddo Letter' (here renamed 'Yaddo, or a month in the country') the same academic may well coin the phrase 'performative privacy' for the mix of raw sincerity, mawkishness, pomp and bad faith that Mahon falls prey to when this strategy fails him. Some of the epistles have lately turned to elegies (as for James Simmons), which asserts another kind of community: where you once had predecessors, you now have predeceasors.

Mahon was epistolizing almost from the start, but it's something he does more and more in his late work. The self-location has, also, a stocktaking dimension to it, where the poet sits and contemplates the brokenness of his life ('Dawn at St Patrick's'), but also the serendipitous, aleatory ways in which other broken things reach him and contribute to new kinds of wholeness. What struck me reading Mahon through once more was that I imagined him as a poet who was always moving from place to place. Looking at it more closely I realized that, in fact, none of his poems are about the actual moving; they're all about the 'having moved'. Hence the tendency to start poems with the 'I sit/stand/lie reading/writing/observing' gambit. Having located himself, like the pin of the school compass dug into the paper, the poet can begin to circumferate.

Baudelaire had his 'Phares', Mahon has his 'Harbour Lights', with all those implications of homecoming and prodigal return that critics picked up on. So much of Mahon is indeed about getting one's bearings, but also about reminding us that the wreckage and detritus, the spume and flotsam, can tell us as much in their way about how to orientate ourselves as any harbour or lighthouse.

72 (Summer 2012)

'I Think Clarity is the Way to Go'

Ahren Warner talks to *Don Paterson*

Ahren Warner: You've said that 'poetic language has two functions; to make things clear and distinct where they weren't, and to join them back up again when they were broken apart. It's a natural function of language, and the way that *language*, certainly, redeems itself'. Paul Muldoon has also talked about a holistic aspect to modern poetics, and you share a common influence in Frost, who you talk of elsewhere as the model of a poet who wrote 'things of immense philosophical subtlety in a language readers can follow'. I wondered if you could speak about the aesthetics, or even ethics – as well as the relationship between – clarity and wholeness in your work?

Don Paterson: There're different issues around clarity, and it's about being honest about what's being communicated just on the simple level of information. The first thing to eliminate is incompetence. The deictic fuck-ups of pronouns, sequence, location, literal and figurative distinction... these things can get lost pretty quickly through being too close to it all. But I do think there's a certain moral obligation towards clarity, because it's an act of communication, isn't it? He said naively. It's two monkeys, and one monkey is trying to say something that's really difficult, and slightly beyond what the language is capable of holding, and is trying to do so by the projection of the principle of equivalence into the syntagm and all that. For that reason alone, I think you're obliged to be as clear as possible. You have a greater obligation to clarity the more complex the idea you're trying to communicate. In terms of the holistic, if your aim is unity and integrity – or at least bringing two ideas together into some kind of genuine synthesis – then you're trying to get, as Hughes says, every word listening to every other word, so the whole structure is self-supporting, a cellular entity. And if you think the point you're making is a moral or ethical one... it strikes me as plainly *un*ethical to present it in language likely to confound the reader. Actually it strikes me as so bleedin' uncontroversial as to be barely worth saying. Though as we know not everyone shares that point of view. Stand up, Geoffrey. (Far more time for J.H. P[rynne] these days, as his language actually honours his project.)

AW: This is also a position that holds a certain relationship to Modernism, of which you've written elsewhere that one of the 'legacies of Modernism' is a historical trend of poets 'making themselves irrelevant' and an unfortunate paradoxical effect of this on current poets as an imperative to be 'interesting' by which, I think, you were referring towards a tendency towards over-accessibility or over-simplification. I wondered about the distinction, for you, between clarity and simplification?

DP: It's a risk. I mean, I think the risk is sounding simple, simplistic – and Frost, for God knows how long, was dismissed for that very reason. He's blatantly *not* simple, or anything like it, but that's the risk. I know I've said this before, but I think there's a kind of fruitful risk in also playing it as close to sentimentality as one dares – and maybe a dumb sort of clarity, and adopting an *almost* pretentious rhetorical height. You fall off the tightrope and make a fool of yourself, but I think you have to risk it. It strikes me that that sort of game is worth playing, because the stakes are a lot higher; potentially you win a lot more in terms of the *force* of what you communicate, the strength of feeling you can share with or elicit from the reader, the coining of speech that is both familiar and radically destabilizing. But you *have* to run the risk of looking like a pretentious dick. An idiot. A sentimental buffoon. Many of our late-mod, non-conformist friends never look so silly, but then they risk very little.

But then again… in terms of the Modernist thing… I've got a lot more sympathy than I did even five years ago, because I've been, y'know, speaking to people. Kinsella is eloquent on these matters. I'm not quite the slave to my own prejudices that I used to be. But I still come back to that idea of what kind of work the poem does. The poem can heal, and the poem can also fracture – but in *both* instances it can present itself as a unity. Its *purpose* can be to fracture – but I think it fractures more effectively when it's a unity, rather than some kind of poem-kit that leaves the reader bleeding and covered in glue before they can even start to read it. There are certain kinds of contemporary practice where the stakes are just too low. It depends how you define 'stakes', but I think if you're trying to *share* stuff with somebody, to move somebody, to propose an idea that we can *speak* about rather than just laboriously parse and unpack, and then be too knackered to do anything else with – if we're using the poem as more than an excuse to have a conversation *about fucking poetry*… I think clarity is the way to go.

AW: You've insisted elsewhere on a kind of unity or complicity between poet and reader. In your T.S. Eliot Lecture, you stated that:

If the aim is just to finish the poem and not publish it, the poet has configured their relation to it imperfectly from the start… Publication – by which I simply mean 'someone else reading your poem' – directly unites the reader and poet, and to read out a line someone else has written in your own voice is to experience a little transmigration of souls…

I wondered if there is a tension, or not, between the argumentative, the discursive and this seeking or production of complicity?

DP: Hopefully not. 'Complicity' hopefully comes through the reader being in a position of overhearing somebody working it through. As opposed to working it through in your own time, away from the piano, and then grandly delivering your lofty findings. Readers hear a voice – a conditional, uncertain voice – with which they can identify and, y'know… follow the same kind of process as the author has experienced it. I think that's where the complicity comes in. It's not a rhetorical trick. I think you have to leave yourself open, when you're writing, to being read in just that way. To be overheard thinking. Being unsure. Conditional. Contradictory. But there's no guarantee, y'know: 'I know what I have given you; I do not know what you have received'. So there's a leap of faith, or there should be. Or rather a leap of trust.

AW: Related to this notion of 'complicity', I'm interested in the role of the everyday, of the objects of the modern world as deployed in your work. I'm thinking here of the 'googling' in your 'Song for Natalie "Tusja" Beridze' or the 'knotted Fetherlite' and 'Keanu Reeves' in your '*from* 1001 Nights'. I'm interested to ask if you see the deployment of everyday objects as a way of invoking complicity?

DP: Well… probably, but I don't know if *complicity* is the right word. I'm all too aware of the function of those contemporary signifiers, and that's the reason they're there, I guess – and that's the reason it's very dangerous to overdo it. What's most 'now' is quickest 'last week'. But to eliminate them, to be tempted too much to the other side, that might lead to a poetry that was so *sub specie aeternitatis* that it was impossible to identify with. You might recruit some future readership who regarded you as a cool, anachronistic Augustan or something – but I think it's safer to be in dialogue with the one you actually have. That lay community who can *actually* tell you you're talking shite. I think the trick is just not to think about it too much. Respond honestly to your environment. If that includes the absolutely contemporary, then fine. But the classic mistake is not trusting yourself. I always think of the end of Mahon's 'Beyond Howth Head' where he changed the last lines: the ones we all committed to memory are 'as I put out the light / on Mailer's *Armies of the Night*', a brilliant line – ties it to a very specific time and place, you know exactly when it was written… but it's also an *eternally* beautiful line. And then of course it's been since revised to 'as I put out the light / on shadows of encroaching night' or something. And no one's gonna tell *me* it's a better line, even Derek, I mean – I'm not *rememorizing* it! It's my poem now! I think the error there was to go for something superficially less time-bound.

AW: Sticking with 'the familiar', I admire your statement, again in your T.S. Eliot Lecture, that

> for a reader to be blown away by the original phrase *it must already be partly familiar to them*, if they are to register the transformation – a point fatally misunderstood by every generation of the avant-garde, which is one reason they are stylistically interchangeable…

It seems to me the risk, the radical complicity of the familiar, and the kind of unthinkable phenomena of affect, is something your work is concerned with (especially in more 'personal' poems such as 'The Thread' or 'The Circle' or even 'Phantom'). I wonder to what extent the designations of 'mainstream' and 'avant-garde' mean anything to you, in general and in relation to the notion of risk?

DP: The big risk is just being understood and being found to be saying nothing. Easier not to be understood. Safer, certainly. But if the original isn't

part-known – then it's mere innovation, and it can't be called advance, because it advances from nowhere. But that strategy means you're subverting the cliché and the received. Which is a dangerous place to hang out, and can leave you sounding merely clichéd, if your calculations are wrong, if you've failed to *advertise* the subversion properly. But lazy readers from both camps don't help either. *Oh I've heard this before.* Actually you really haven't. It just sounds like you have.

AW: I wondered if we could talk more specifically about this notion of 'risk'. Again in your T.S. Eliot Lecture, you said that

> risk is also writing with real feeling, as Frost did, while somehow avoiding sentimentality; simplicity, as Cavafy did, and somehow avoiding artlessness; daring to be prophetic, as Rilke did, and miraculously avoiding pretentiousness; writing with real originality, as Dickinson did, while somehow avoiding cliché…

It seems that, here, the notion of 'risk' is divorced from 'experiment', that it is more to do with the force of an artwork than form? How would you think about the relationship between risk and technique, or form?

DP: 'Risk' is a big word and you're right, formally I'm very conservative, so there's no 'risk' involved at that level, but I don't think that's the word to use anyway. I think it's totally inappropriate. Yep – it's to do with force, the speech act and its consequence, including personal consequence. Unfortunately it is a word we do sometimes use in that context – as if there were any sexy virtue in experiment for its own sake, which I just don't believe. I mean – so you've done a homophonic translation of Cavafy in three-letter words and substituted every noun for one four entries along in the dictionary – big fuckin' deal. It's kids' stuff, only kids wouldn't trouble themselves with it because Minecraft is far more fun and creative. Wee word games.

AW: And this is a certain notion of aesthetic 'force'

if you like, force that's not created through structure – though it's facilitated by it – and it's related to a specific notion of what art should do.

DP: Yeah. Your *reputation* should be risked. The reader's mental health should be at risk. Their sleep should be at risk. Their unchallenged assumptions about the world should be at risk. You should risk it *not coming off*, y'know. As opposed to risking what? Boring the reader? Losing the reader? Is that a risk? I'm not sure that qualifies. And I don't think form can be risky in itself.

AW: The stakes of form, in this context, are too low?

DP: That's the point, it's a low stakes game. All form. Meaningless. It's like when one is called 'a lover of the sonnet form'. But I'm indifferent towards the sonnet. It's what goes into it. Look at New Formalism, the promotion of form to an intrinsic *virtue*: I mean give me Keston going all text-puppet any day of the week. The experimental stuff is fun, all that syntactic disjunction and competing jargons… but it results in poetry that's really very conservative in content, as evidenced by the fact that it hasn't changed much for a hundred years. It's like real hardcore squeaky-bonk free jazz. It's sounded like that since the mid-sixties, because it's a negatively defined aesthetic. No heads, no long melodic passages, no structure that isn't soon dismantled, and so on. That's grand, though. I used to play it for a living, and it can be very beautiful – but despite the fact it's allowed to *think* of itself as radical on account of ninety-nine per cent of folk totally *hating* it, it's the most painfully conservative and rulebound music on the planet. It's virtually a classical form. So is the literary avant-garde. Certainly it has all the authorial *anonymity* of classicism. But that's all fine. Live and let live. At least it's identifiably *poetry*.

AW: Previously, you've downplayed the *New Gen* promotion, writing that you 'think the people who came through and found themselves a readership would have done anyway', which is probably true. Yet, a lot of people would say that, regardless of the promotional side of things, a lot of those poets – and others not involved in *New Gen* – maintain a certain cogency or poetic coherency as a grouping. Do you think that would be fair or accurate still?

DP: Yeah, sort of, partly I think it was just a good generation, and it's hard to say what that was down to. We had really good workshop practices that were brutally competitive, and I think that was one factor. It raised everyone's game. I think that's what tends to happen. You get a few really good people coming along – O'Brien and Shapcott, the very slightly older members of that sort of group – they set the bar really quite high. Y'know, it's like Swedish tennis, you get a couple of these guys playing at that level in the domestic game, and you think *Jesus, I've got to get my shit together.* I really believe that healthy competition is a very good thing. My worry is that certain types of workshop practice got fossilized very quickly and had the opposite effect, and we're maybe guilty there. But we spent a long, long, long time working on these lines, ready for next Thursday when you'd all meet in The Lamb or whatever and you got your poem ripped to shreds. '*Kids these days*' seem to spend all their time writing blogs and speaking about… not even poetry: they *think* they're talking about poetry, but they're mostly talking po-biz, or bitching about other poets, and it's like, *No! Just write it.* Spend time just staring at the line for another three years until it comes good on you. Not your blog. There's an awful lot of poetry-talk on Facebook and Twitter that seems to have leached or siphoned off the energy that should have gone into the poem. And I think it's workshop culture that's been to blame for that… it led to the illusion of this being a *career*. Christ I'm sounding so *old*. Fucking *New* Gen. There's a laugh.

AW: Related to this I wondered about a tension in your statement that poetry 'is certainly a craft that could be acquired, but it's useless unless you have talent as a poet. So if you don't have a talent, there's no point in polishing your craft, there's no point in being a competent versifier'. In terms of Creative Writing courses, I mean what is the ethic of teaching those students who have no or little talent?

DP: Well, the first thing to say is that I don't really believe in 'Creative Writing'; I'm really trying my best to get the term off the books, because my colleagues at St Andrews are brilliant scholars, and *they're* creative writers too, so it's a ridiculous distinction. All I teach is poetry, and poetic composition. But you've gotta watch out, you're absolutely right. I mean what's the point of teaching basic competence to people who perhaps don't have any particular talent? It's wasting their time. It's a vale of tears for most poets, y'know, so you don't want to encourage *anybody* into that way of living unless they've got the talent for it. And then there's the whole Ponzi scheme aspect. What are you going to do with this qualification except teach Creative Writing? Because no *editor* is going to be impressed with your postgraduate qualification. It's a teaching qualification, and we have to start making it one. I don't know, I do believe strongly in the one-year Masters, if it's well structured and students are sufficiently talented, as a way of embarking on that formal apprenticeship in a structured way.

AW: I wanted to finish by talking about the long, penultimate poem of *Rain*, 'Phantom', which is dedicated to Michael Donaghy. There's much we could talk about in the poem, but I wanted pick up on those lines 'just plot a course between the Orphic oak / and fuck 'em all if they can't take a joke'. To some extent, this seems a summation of various positions you've espoused in texts we've discussed: the importance of the lyrical, the imperative to sentiment, to emotion or affect as well as a self-deprecating stubbornness. And, of course, here it's Donaghy's voice directing you. I wonder really about his influence on your aesthetics?

DP: Hugely influential, but as a man as much as a poet. But he had something that I very much wanted for my own verse. I don't think I got it, but I got something else in trying. But that was always Mikey's thing, y'know, if you don't entertain first, you don't get to first base, because nobody is listening. I think it's that simple. And also that thing about risk again; he sought it often. Trouble is his poems are often misread as little performances – but the interdependence of their elements, like that self-supporting mathematical bridge in Cambridge, their harmonic complexity… once you see what he's actually doing, it's like Donne, but with a heavy layer of naturalism. They are *ridiculously* complex poems, and anyone who thinks they're simple hasn't read them right, and has confused their relaxed delivery with a similarly laid-back approach to their composition. He worked like a *demon* to sound that casual. You learn to trust, as you do with Muldoon, that everything is there for a structural reason. But it has to be play too – and his wasn't play in any kind of postmodern, ludic and dry way. It was *genuine* play, for the sheer joy of it. I think there's a lot to be won there. A lot of trust to be won. Steering between the joke and the 'tall tree in the ear' is just 'play for mortal stakes' again. And on a purely manipulative level, it's the old Ivor Cutler thing: 'first I get them laughing, and when their mouth's open, I pour in the poison'.

74 (Spring 2013)

Index of Contributors

poetry london
NEWSLETTER

Poems:
Riordan, Wicks,
Copus, Markham,
Burnside

Reviews:
Riordan on
Hughes, Hadari
on Translating
Ahkmatova,
Anthony on
Duran, Baker on
Simic.

national poetry day issue

autumn issue oct '95
volume number five
NUMBER II

LONDON
ARTS BOARD

POETRY LONDON
£3.50   NEWSLETTER   AUTUMN 1996 • 25

UNDER
ROUN

GOING UNDERGROUND Poems on the Underground celebrates
ten years of bringing poems to passengers

THE LONG PALE CORRIDOR Thomas Lynch on bereavement

BURIED WATERS Poems by Julian Turner, Peter Porter,
Martha Kapos, John Harvey, Pauline Stainer and others

LONDON
ARTS BOARD   **THROUGH THE EUROTUNNEL** Katherine Gallagher goes French.
Verlaine translations by Carl Morse

MIMI KHALVATI GOES WORKSHOPPING + LOADS OF LISTINGS

POETRY LONDON
£3.50   SUMMER 2000 • 36

GREEN MUSIC AND A SINGING SUN Poems by Jaan Kaplinski
+ Moniza Alvi + Peter Redgrove + Penelope Shuttle + Elizabeth Jennings
+ Ken Smith + James Harpur

RED ROCK, RUSSIAN GOLD Ciaran Carson on Redgrove and
Shuttle + Feinstein's Tsvetaeva, Feinstein's Pushkin, Feinstein's Feinstein

Funded by
THE
ARTS
COUNCIL
OF ENGLAND   **JO SHAPCOTT INTERVIEWED** + Reviews of Les Murray,
Pauline Stainer, C.K. Williams, Thom Gunn, Sappho

LONDON
ARTS BOARD

SUMMER LISTINGS + POETRY INTERNATIONAL SNEAK PREVIEW

AUTUMN 2000   37   £3.50

poetry london

**ROBERT MINHINNICK
DANCES WITH DNA**

Poems by
Robert Minhinnick
Ruth Padel
John Hartley Williams
Matthew Francis
Gillian Allnutt
Virgil Suárez
Judith Barrington

**DAVID CONSTANTINE
REVIEWS GLÜCK & KHALVATI**

Kleinzahler on Bunting
O'Donoghue on Sweeney

**LISTINGS: HOW TO SURVIVE
THE WINTER**

LONDON
ARTS BOARD   Funded by
THE
ARTS
COUNCIL
OF ENGLAND

RICHARD WILBUR — A POET TO KNOW BETTER, BY D. M. BLACK

SUMMER 2004 | 48 | £5.00

poetry london

TIME'S CHILDREN

Poems by Mark Doty

Ruth Padel

John Kinsella

Katherine Pierpoint

Maurice Manning

Valerie Mejer

RICHARD KING VISITS BOLLOCKSHIRE & BERMUDAPEST

Roddy Lumsden goes for a batch of first collections

OH, MURIEL RUKEYSER — WE SURE DO NEED YOU NOW!

AUTUMN 2005 | 52 | £5.00

poetry london

RUNNING FOR HOME

Poems by

Simon Armitage

Leontia Flynn

Seamus Heaney

Valerio Magrelli

Kathryn Simmonds

2005 COMPETITION WINNERS

KATHRYN MARIS HAILS THE GENIUS OF ANNE STEVENSON

Reviews of Kinsella, Lumsden, Petit, Yang Lian, & pamphlets

JAMIE MCKENDRICK PROFILES MONTALE WHOSE STATURE FILLS THE PIAZZA

Summer 2007 no.57 £5.00

poetry london

Laff-in-the-Dark

Poems by

Chase Twichell

and

Ciaran Carson
Jamie McKendrick
Markus Lloyd

Hacker's pleasure in Bishop's unpublished poems

Peter Porter's powerful celebration of Auden

Plus reviews of Feinstein, Duhig, Longley and Nagra

Martyn Crucefix scorns Ashbery's meaningless poems

SPRING 2009 NO. 62 / £6

poetry london

ANNOUNCING POETRY LONDON COMPETITION 2009

Jagirs of Gold

Poems by

Daljit Nagra

Sinéad Morrissey
John Kinsella
Helen Farish

Strange Fruit
Luke Kennard on Francis Ponge

Szirtes at Sixty, Heaney at Seventy

Plus reviews of
Agbabi, Bennet, Maxwell and Flynn

AUTUMN 2010 NO.67 / £6

poetry london

2010
COMPETITION
WINNERS

A hopeful & hopeless reckoning

Poems by
Fred D'Aguiar

Medbh McGuckian
Sean O'Brien
Annie Freud

Plain heaven
George Szirtes on Peter Porter

With regrets
Eva Salzman on Derek Walcott

Plus reviews of
Glück, Mackinnon, Shapcott and Stammers

AUTUMN 2011 NO.70 / £8

poetry london

2011
COMPETITION
WINNERS

logging in Hades

Poems by
Helen Farish

Paul Durcan
Kathleen Jamie
Luke Kennard

Mulberry and oleander
Martyn Crucefix on Iraq
in recent poetry

Beyond performance
Fred d'Aguiar on Jean 'Binta'
Breeze and Mutabaruka

Plus reviews of
Longley, O'Brien,
Cope and Satyamurti

SPRING 2012 NO.71 / £8

poetry london

ANNOUNCING
POETRY LONDON
COMPETITION
2012

Definite Signs

Poems by
Julia Copus

Jane Hirshfield
Michael Symmons Roberts
Vicki Feaver

Walking around an enigma
George Szirtes on Tomas Tranströmer

Truth and dare
An interview with Christopher Reid

Plus reviews by
Alison Brackenbury, W N Herbert,
Bernard O'Donoghue and Peter Robinson

AUTUMN 2013 NO.76 / £8

poetry london

2013
COMPETITION
WINNERS

Another body

Poems by
Matthew Dickman

Christopher Middleton
Rachael Allen
David Harsent

Going Through the Fire
Daljit Nagra talks to Clare Pollard

Double, Double...
Luke Kennard on WH Herbert's *Omnesia*

Plus reviews of
John Agard, Alison Brackenbury,
Michael Symmons Roberts and
Keston Sutherland

SUPPORT FOR POETRY LONDON

At *Poetry London* we aim to attract and publish the best new work in contemporary poetry from the UK and across the world. We regularly give one third of the poetry pages to poets who have yet to publish a first collection. The reviews pages feature new names alongside those of distinguished writers. As Ruth Padel has put it, 'What they have in common is their excellence'.

All of this is widely known to poets and poetry readers across the UK. What may be less well known about *Poetry London* is that it is almost unique among major poetry magazines in that it survives without the backing of a press, or any other organisation or owner. We are a small charitable organisation working on a minimal budget and dependent on funding from Arts Council England.

The Best of Poetry London has got off the ground by virtue of the huge generosity of its contributors who have donated their work free of charge. We are also enormously grateful to each of their publishers who have, without exception, waived their usual permission fees in order to enable this project to go ahead.

We are especially grateful to Carcanet Press, which, while waiving permission fees for its own poets selected for the anthology, is also donating the profits from sales to *Poetry London* to help to safeguard its future.

You can help *Poetry London* by becoming a subscriber! Go to our website at www.poetrylondon.co.uk, write to our office: Poetry London, The Albany, Douglas Way, Deptford, London, SE8 4AG, or phone 020 8691 7260.

You can help *Poetry London* by giving a donation via our website or at our office!

'The magazine is a medley of sharp, dim, ironic and appreciative voices..and seems unlikely to go stale.'

Poetry Review

'Poetry London Newsletter is South-East England's foremost poetry magazine, with an intelligent, wide-ranging feel to it and an extensive review section and listings guide. It is published three times a year.'

Eastside Bookshop.

ISSN 0953-766X

9 770953 766025

£3.50